Rick Stein's

French Odyssey

Rick Stein's
French Odyssey

Over 100 New Recipes Inspired by the Flavours of France

Food photography by James Murphy with food styling by Debbie Major Location photography by Craig Easton

This book is published to accompany the television series entitled *Rick Stein's French Odyssey*.
The series was produced for BBC Television by Denham Productions.
Producer and Director: David Pritchard
Assistant Producer: Arezoo Farahzad
Executive Producer for the BBC: Tom Archer

First published by BBC Books in 2005
Reprinted 2005
BBC Worldwide Limited
80 Wood Lane
London W12 0TT

ISBN 0 563 52213 5

Commissioning Editor: Vivien Bowler
Project Editor: Mari Roberts
Designer: Lisa Pettibone
Stylist: Antonia Gaunt
Map Illustration: Ann Ramsbottom
Production Controller: Kenneth McKay

Set in Bodoni and Univers
Colour separations by Butler and Tanner Origination
Printed and bound in Great Britain by Butler and Tanner Limited, Frome and London

Acknowledgements

I would like to thank Debbie Major, who has contributed a vast amount to this book both in writing up and testing recipes and in cooking the food for photography. I would also like to thank my Commissioning Editor, Viv Bowler, who has once again quietly kept the project on course as well as being a major influence on the shape of the whole book. I've now created six books with Debbie, Viv and photographer James Murphy, testimony to how much I value them. I have also worked with landscape photographer Craig Easton for the last four books, evidence of how I admire his choice of locations to illustrate my books. I love the design of the book by Lisa Pettibone and the cover by Henry Steadman, and I have been extremely well looked after editorially by Mari Roberts. The TV series that accompanies this has been a vitally important influence on the book, and for this I would like to thank Producer/Director David Pritchard, Assistant Producer Arezoo Farahzad, Second Director Bernard Hall, Cameraman Chris Topliss and Sound Engineer Pete Underwood. A word of thanks to Matthew Stevens, our fish merchant at The Seafood Restaurant, who supplied perfectly fresh seafood for testing the recipes, and David West of Sway in Lymington, Debbie's brother-in-law, who must be one of the best local butchers around. And last but not least, enormous thanks to Viv Taylor, my PA, who has managed my time with gritty determination, and my girlfriend, Sarah, who lent us her kitchen in Sydney to finish testing the recipes in the Australian summer.

Notes on the recipes

- All teaspoon and tablespoon measurements are level unless otherwise stated and are based on measuring spoons: 1 teaspoon = 5 ml and 1 tablespoon = 15 ml.
- All recipes have been tested in a conventional oven. For a fan oven, reduce the temperature by about 20°C. I always test with an oven thermometer before cooking.
- Free-range eggs are recommended in all recipes. Recipes with raw or lightly cooked eggs should be avoided by anyone who is pregnant or in a vulnerable health group.

Contents

Notes from a journey

It might have been sensible to close the little top window at the front of my cottage in Padstow when I left at 5.30 a.m. on Monday 7 June for the ferry terminal at Plymouth. A week later, on the canal boat from Bordeaux to Marseille, I found out someone had tried to squeeze through it, but had been surprised by one of my restaurant chefs rolling home at 3 a.m. and had run off down the road, followed closely, apparently, by his lurcher dog.

It was overexcitement, I'm afraid. I was too busy packing my Michelin guide, well-thumbed copy of Elizabeth David's *French Provincial Cooking*, a CD called *Learn French Now!* and maps of Charente-Maritime, Bordeaux, Gascony, the Languedoc and Provence. I had a little book on the Canal du Midi by a rather pedantic yachtsman who preferred the canal system to get to the Mediterranean rather than sailing round Spain and Portugal. My prized possession, though, was a treasured copy of Caroline Conran's *Under the Sun*, in which she describes the complete euphoria of leaving 1960s' London and driving the plane-tree-lined straight roads all the way to Saint Tropez. As she pointed out, the food from the south is simple to make and relies on a

harmony of flavours rather than a lot of decoration or extravagant ingredients. 'The French call it *cuisine de terroir*,' she wrote, and that was what I was looking for, the sort of food that has made Italy so popular but which I knew I could also find in the French Midi.

I packed a couple of knives, too, hoping to do some cooking on the way, and some Proust, Alexandre Dumas, Montagne, and DVDs of *Jean de Florette* and *Manon des Sources*, foolishly thinking I would have plenty of time on the long voyage south to catch up on relevant reading and watch a couple of atmospheric films of Provençal peasant life.

This was the start of another food journey, a French odyssey. David Pritchard, the producer I work with, and I had decided to make the trip some months before. We had suggested the idea of a voyage of food discovery through southern France to the BBC, who seemed interested but asked for a written outline. On a paper tablecloth in Le Quartier Vert, a restaurant near the BBC in Whiteladies Road, Bristol, David drew a map of southern France. He put in the canal system we were going to travel along: the Canal Latéral à la Garonne, the Canal du Midi

and the Canal du Rhône à Marseille. Then he drew pictures of various food areas – a rather rudimentary duck here with the comment 'foie gras country', and a sheep there, 'brebis cheese from these marsh sheep near Pouillac'. Here 'an Aussie flying winemaker makes great Viognier', down on the Mediterranean 'étang de Thau oysters growing on stakes', and in another place 'Rick has posh Sauternes-maker chum'. Then he spilt a little red wine on it, borrowed a fag and made a couple of cigarette burns, folded the tablecloth and posted it to the boss at the BBC.

Next day it seemed like a bit of lunchtime euphoria and maybe they wouldn't enjoy our sense of humour, but they did, though they asked for a more conventional treatment as well.

When I picked up that phone message about my house, I was out fishing for shad in the Garonne, some 20 kilometres east of Bordeaux, with fisherman Alain Penichon. We had boarded our first canal boat the day before at Bègles, Bordeaux. Named the *Rosa*, it was 130 feet long, slept eight and had a crew of three. Boarding the barge, as they are called, was astonishing. I had been used to

British canal boats, long and very narrow, where you have to pull your tummy in when anyone passes you. Here was luxurious accommodation: rooms with double beds and bathrooms, and air-conditioning too – well, sometimes. The main cabin was spacious with sofas and a big dining table and a small bar, behind which I determinedly hung a painting of Chalky, my Jack Russell. We had hoped to take him with us. He likes being on the water and would have been great at chasing ducks, but sadly we hadn't had him computer-chipped in time, and the vet back home said he was a bit old anyway.

And I was off fishing for legendary shad. We caught a dozen handsome deep-bodied silver fish using a light net cast out into the current. The softness of the light, the weedy smell and the warm brown river were captivating, quite unlike sea fishing. Alain, like all the river fishermen I met, was quiet, relaxed, content to watch the river flow. We were going to take these fish back to Alain's house on the banks of the river and cook them over vine prunings. A vine-pruning barbecue in the Bordelaise: of such things are dreams made. It wasn't just the fragrant smoky steaks of fish, but a frying pan

Padstow

Plymouth

Roscoff

Nantes

La Rochelle

Ile dOlé ron

Bordeaux

Atlantic Ocean

Toulouse

Marseille

Mediterranean Sea

9

filled with sandy pommes sarladaise cooked in goose fat with a persillade of parsley and garlic, and a sauce gribiche of chopped egg yolks, capers, parsley and red wine vinegar – the perfect accompaniment. Then, to finish, a tart of sliced caramelized apples. A local Bordeaux red, Domaine de Labache, was a perfect fit. I had to pinch myself, even with that mobile-phone message about my house.

That night we reached the beginning of the Canal Latéral à la Garonne, which runs beside the river all the way from Bordeaux to Toulouse, built because much

of the river is too shallow for barging. I had to become used to the word barging – or, more accurately, bargin'. The crew of the *Rosa*, Bernard, Michel and Julie, were French and formal and so much of the secret life of bargin' was at that stage unknown to us.

Bernard, we soon learnt, ran a very tight ship, but the extraordinary formality of the meals he cooked and served was one of the most revealing parts of the trip, revealing about the difference between the British and French attitude to food. Julie described a visit to a pen-friend in

Grimsby a couple of years previously as being very enjoyable, but extraordinary in that the whole family seemed to be constantly watching TV and eating while they did so. Bernard's lunches and dinners were always four courses, always taken at a leisurely pace and always just enough and no more. There is a French saying to the effect that one should always leave the table wanting more. That is why French women don't get fat – they take their time about eating. I did a little chat to the DVC camera towards the end of the voyage, an inspired idea of David's: ten

The Canal du Midi near Argeliers between Carcassonne and Béziers

large duck breasts from birds reared for foie gras, with a faint flavour of that delectable luxury. It's not really a criticism to say he was pretty parsimonious, too. It goes, I think, with a proper sense of economy in cooking. The first course was always a small quantity of soup, a thin slice of tart or salad. On one occasion he produced a salad of sliced Quercy melons, Marmande tomatoes and cucumber with some crumbled brebis, a sheep's milk cheese – summer in Gascony on a plate.

The next course would be a simple piece of fish or meat, again modest in size, followed every day by at least three cheeses, which Bernard would slice with the skill of a Japanese sashimi chef, and which he would deliver individually and with a running commentary, often of donnish anecdotes about the cheeses, such as the mould in the caves of Roquefort, the carrot juice giving the extraordinary orange colour in Mimolette, or the fact that the word 'crottins', for the little disc-shaped goat's cheeses, comes from their resemblance to goat's droppings.

The sweet would be maybe a local tarte aux pommes from a patisserie near the canal, or a crème caramel, again from a local shop. Often Bernard would only make one course, but that is another thing so different in France – the availability in any nearby small town of shops that specialize in really good quality cooked food. Doing all the cooking for these regular four-course meals would be both unthinkable and unnecessary. Why make things that you can buy almost better locally?

things we like about France. Number one, of course, was the women – their style, their elegance in dress at whatever age – but number two was the simple fact that everything stops for lunch. Other things were: there are very few signs telling you what to do or not to do, and, surprisingly perhaps, after a month or two there you realize that the French, certainly in the south, are actually nice.

What Bernard cooked for us was not particularly unusual: artichokes with vinaigrette, sautéed eel with persillade, an onion tart, grilled magret de canard – the

But I wasn't quite so happy with the sense of economy with the wines. On most nights, David wondered if we would be presented with yet another rusty wine, for the reds were often brown and old, and the whites dull and flat. He thought they had been stored next to the boat's engine for too long. I don't know if Bernard thought he was treating us as ignorant Britons and getting rid of some wines that frankly should have gone into the vinegar barrel, or if he genuinely thought he was giving us hallowed old bottles. I do know that on a research trip earlier that year with my girlfriend Sarah, we went to a restaurant in Auvillar famed for its regional wines only to find there was not a white on the list less than four years old. In contrast, most of the wines on my restaurant list, with the exception of some expensive Burgundies or Bordeaux and a few others, are no more than two years old, since most whites are best drunk within a year or two of making.

The trip made me realize that there is an awful lot of extremely ordinary wine in France. This year 284 million bottles of rusty Bordelaise wine have been turned into industrial alcohol. It's a bit like British cars in the early seventies, swept inevitably away by better products from elsewhere. (Remember the Allegro or the Montego?) Give me a bottle of Cricket Pitch, Cloudy Bay or Mad Fish any day.

Nevertheless, I still think that the French make the best wine in the world. Earlier on, when we were travelling down from Roscoff in the Land-Rover before we joined the barge, we stopped off at Vallet, just south of Nantes, to meet our Muscadet producer, Jean-Ernest Sauvion. When we arrived, Jean-Ernest came out of the chateau to greet us and immediately

11

suggested a cold glass of Château du Cléray, his Muscadet. We sat in the shade of a leafy tree and I enjoyed the slight unkemptness of the grass – the French don't really have lawns round their houses, just grass. His PR and marketing manager Roselyne sat down too, needless to say wonderfully elegantly dressed, and as we sat in easy chairs on a hot summer afternoon just across from the slightly faded chateau with peeling shutters in pale green, a shade even the National Trust couldn't match, I was moved to comment on the extraordinary complexity of that lovely wine: its Melon de Bourgogne taste, its freshness, its clarity. Later we drank more in the dining room with langoustines and mayonnaise, then with poached sea bass and the local butter, wine vinegar and shallot sauce, beurre blanc Nantais, and finally a slightly sweet old botrytis version with raspberries and crème fraîche.

I awoke early next morning in the chateau and looked through the half-opened shutters past a tall beech tree over straight green lines of vines on a soft cloud-less summer morning and thought, France really is *la belle*.

Meanwhile, life on the *Rosa* became a routine. Both barges we travelled on, this and later the *Anjodi*, were long and wide. The eight passengers slept at the bow in four cabins. Life was serene; the old girl chugged along at about 4 miles an hour. These boats are converted cargo barges, their hulls sixty to eighty years old. Barge owners tend to grow geraniums in pots along the railings and put easy chairs and umbrellas on the decks. There you relax as the barge meanders along through arcades of green shade from the over-hanging plane or oak trees, planted to keep the sun off the animals in the days of horse-power. It's a constantly changing vista: sometimes a ruined chateau, then a

distant village with church and spire, then yellow fields of corn and endless rows of vines running up the hills beyond. All the time you pass antiquated pumps sucking water out of the canal to irrigate the fields. Some of the bridges are so low you have to duck to go under them. There's often somebody fishing just by the bridge. Sometimes, in the cities, there are out-of-work youths smoking and drinking cans of lager.

I wouldn't fancy the fish from the canal. I jumped in once, from the *Anjodi*, to help the skipper remove a nest of rope, wire and, bizarrely, women's tights from the propeller. The water was cleaner than it looked, sort of grey-green, like dish-washing water. There's no sewage, but the hundreds of uniform white plastic boats on hire up and down the journey, and universally known as Noddy boats, surely churn out a lot of washing-up water. On a barge, you are the correct form of canal

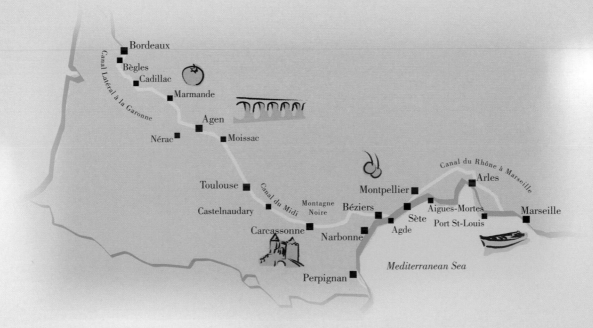

transport, and you feel superior to those over-cheerful Noddy-boaters getting in the way. It's total bliss.

Canal life is fantastic. Mind you, you do hear of complaints about the state of some of the canals in France. On one stretch of the Canal Latéral, we saw a lot of old lock-owners' houses that had been left to fall to ruin. We looked over one, a substantial house with the front door hanging off a hinge and plaster falling off an upstairs ceiling, and the remnants of wallpaper with tiny blue flowers in what must have been the bathroom. The back of the house was built into the slope up to the stables, long since empty but once accommodating the canal horses, and a fence and vines stretched into the distance as far as you could see. In a way, parts of the canal system in disrepair add romance to the journey. It's a bit like the Lost Gardens of Heligan in Cornwall, parts of which are still not reclaimed – and long may they remain so.

Coming into a village is particularly easy on the eye. The first two canals, the Canal Latéral and then the Canal du Midi, were built when the waterways were the deluxe form of transport, so that unlike entering a modern town either by train past back gardens, graffiti-daubed walls and rusty factories or by road past garish blocks of new industrial estates, by canal you go through the best bits: past chateaus and under elegant bridges and alongside towpaths with pretty houses right into the centre. In Toulouse, where we would change from the *Rosa* to the *Anjodi*, the canal basin is pleasantly close to the Victor Hugo market in the middle of the city.

The Canal du Midi is now a wonder of the world. It was built between 1667 and 1681, and paved the way for the industrial revolution in France. The care its creator, Pierre-Paul Riquet, took in the design and the way it blends with its surroundings turned a technical achievement into a work of art. The oval-shaped locks are a visual delight to match any sculpture. Every time we entered on the *Anjodi*, they made us smile. The French have the same reverence for Riquet that we have for Isambard Kingdom Brunel. Everything he built has an uplifting quality: not only the locks, but the bridges over the canal, too, and the aqueducts that carry the canal over a river. He built a reservoir in the Montagne Noire to feed the system that finally connected *les deux mers* – the

Ecluses de Fonserannes, Béziers – a flight of nine locks on the Canal du Midi

Atlantic with the Mediterranean – and this has the same feeling of permanence and elegance.

I hope this book does wonders for barging holidays on these canals. It's not just the laid-back nature of the travel, but also that it's so interesting. There's the interaction with lock keepers, for example. I suppose on average you need to go through a lock an hour. Some keepers are dour with a job to do and a whiff of disdain for the Noddy-boaters; others are students. I particularly remember a pretty girl who ran a double lock and whizzed between the two on a moped. Sometimes the keepers sell things, such as food, or on one occasion a series of differently

sized wooden chickens on springs. There are restaurants, too, not as many as you'd think, but one in particular stands out: just outside Agen, with a lively cook called Vetou. She cooked a beautiful magret de canard for us, with a really good red wine sauce made from a Côtes du Marmandais from the Cave Co-operative de Cocument, some prunes and a little chocolate.

Restaurants in France are the subject of much argument. It is common to hear British people bemoaning the drop in standards. Everyone remembers an excellent tomato salad, steak frites and crème caramel they got for £2.50 in the old days. I can report that you can still eat better in France than almost anywhere in the world,

but you need to watch out. It's often the case that the less you pay for a meal, the better it is. I can think of a simple dish of clams in a velouté, garlic and parsley sauce we had at Les Grillardines, a roadside café just by the causeway to the mainland on the Ile d'Oléron near La Rochelle. And in Brittany, near Rennes, there was a routière, a truck-stop restaurant, where we had good hors d'oeuvres carrot salad with tomato, chicory, parsley and vinaigrette, beetroot with the same dressing and a touch of garlic, a local rabbit terrine with a few cornichons (gherkins), then a plate of eels stewed in local cider and a pitcher of the same to go with it – that lovely Breton cider, deep yellow with a warm sweet

16

bouquet of soft raisins but dry to the taste with a good element of tannin too.

Another meal, a thick, dark fish soup in a seafood restaurant in Agde on the final stretch of the Hérault river before it runs into the Mediterranean, just near the sombre black granite twelfth-century cathedral. We were packed in at long tables and an enormous tureen of the soup was produced: deep brown, flavoured with North African harissa, and with piles of French bread and rouille to float in it. The wine was a rugged rosé, the sort of thing that would taste quite unpalatable back home.

Perhaps my fondest memory, though, of incredibly inexpensive eating was the

station buffet in Agen. We arrived there on the *Rosa* by night, crossing over the spectacular aqueduct across the Tarn, and the next morning headed to the station buffet for an early lunch. I had been before and completely enjoyed the twelve-euro menu, which started, unbelievably, with foie gras salad, then chargrilled tenderloins of magret: those little contra fillets that cling to the main breast. I could also have had a salad of confit de gésiers instead of my foie gras: duck gizzards, salted and slow-cooked in duck fat, then sliced and served cold. Or I could have had a bavette of skirt steak, a long cut they normally top with shallots fried till brown and a deep bordelaise

Previous page: The Canal du Midi
Above: La Cité de Carcassonne: the old medieval walled town surrounded by vineyards

sauce. In Britain we turn our noses up at such cuts since they are a bit tough, but in France, along with the locals, we enjoyed their chewy flavour with frites. Dessert and a pichet of red wine were included in the price. We waited until a train arrived on the way to Marseille, and I did a little piece to camera imagining what similar delights one could expect from an English station buffet: cheese and mayonnaise sandwiches, a Cornish pasty, perhaps to be reheated in a microwave, maybe a similarly reheatable sausage roll. I also mentioned that the train would take its passengers to our destination in a few hours; by barge we were still weeks away.

We made our way from Agen to Toulouse, stopping briefly at Moissac. On a number of occasions we came across food I could not give a recipe for in this book because the ingredients would be impossible to get at home. In Bordeaux, for example, there's a fabulous restaurant called La Tupina, in rue Port de la Monnaie right near the Gironde. It is famous for its open-hearth cooking and excellent wine list of carefully chosen Bordeaux. A log fire burns summer and winter, and chicken and other meat and game roasts in front of it on spits driven by chains and clockwork. They cook chips in duck fat and beautiful côtes de boeuf on little grill ledges, and they also use duck fat to fry pig's chitterlings cut into 4-centimetre sections, which they season with salt and pepper and sprinkle with parsley. They are called tricandilles grésillent, and they taste a bit like andouillettes. I love them, but you'd never find them here in the UK. In Moissac, just by the river Tarn, there's a restaurant called Le Pont Napoleon. Here chef Michel Dussau takes a whole fresh foie gras and sautés it in a little duck fat in a big copper pan. He adds red Banyuls wine and fresh cherry coulis and cooks the foie gras for 20 minutes, then he removes it and keeps it warm and makes a sauce with the cooking juices, more cherry coulis and chicken stock. He reduces that right down and gently cooks some freshly stoned cherries, slices of peach and pear in the sauce, then serves the whole foie gras, still weighing about 700 grams, sliced, with some of the sauce and some of the fruit. It is sensational – the fresh and still tart fruit cuts through

the richness of the foie gras and you feel you are eating something you could never recreate.

At Toulouse we remarked on the perfection of the sausages at the covered market, as well as the wonderful shops and sophisticated feeling of this red-brick university town. I went into a fish frenzy at the market, where the quality and variety were excellent and, interestingly, there were equal quantities of Atlantic and Mediterranean fish.

The next stop was Castelnaudary, and the search for a perfect cassoulet. First we visited the French Foreign Legion to see what they eat in their mess. It was confit of duck with a very nice salad and sarladaise potatoes. The Foreign Legionnaires are in very good shape. I noted that Coca-Cola comes in wine-glass-size cups, not the buckets we now get back home. We watched their parade and their slow, menacing march into battle, which they accompany with the singing of a dirge. It was very moving; almost an anticipation of death.

Next we ate cassoulet, lots of it, at the Hotel de France. It was very good but needed lots of red wine to wash it down. We filmed at a cassoulet festival that evening, interviewing a robed celebrant who says he wouldn't touch cassoulet in the summer months – far too filling.

The next morning we went to see a legendary winemaker at Badens called Pierre Cros, with an Australian wine-writer friend of mine called Peter Forrestal. I'd mentioned to Peter one time in Australia that I was making a TV series in France and would like an Australian view of French wine. He had heard of Pierre, the winemaker from Minervois who was making a legendary wine from

the Carignan grape called Domaine Cros Minervois Vieilles Vignes. He'd had some shipped out to Perth, and raved about it. The famous American winemaker Robert Parker had given the 1998 wine 90 out of 100 and described it as: 'Medium-to-full-bodied and velvety-textured, it boasts penetrating red/black cherry, blueberry and licorice flavors in its powerful, jammy personality.' Well, it might have been all that, but it was also a shining example of the quality of wine that now comes out of the Languedoc. Given the freedom that this part of France has to use whatever grapes it likes, it would be interesting if some other parts might be similarly free to produce more interesting wine than that prescribed by the Appellation Contrôlé system, where the precise grape content of the wine is laid down. These days, single varietals like Pierre Cros's are also more attractive to those brought up on New World wines. A Chardonnay du Pays d'Oc is much clearer than a Mâcon Clessé, though both are made with the same grape.

I remember that day with great affection. I can still see Pierre standing in his vineyard filled with gnarled and twisted hundred-year-old Carignan vines explaining why the roots of vines as old as this extract so much 'terroir' flavour from the ground. He had a friend with him that day who was keen to promote his band, Zanda, and had artfully left copies of his CD lying around the vinery. I took one back to the *Anjodi* and stuck on the title track, 'Le Temps de Rien', and suddenly we had a vital part of the whole TV series there: it is nonchalant travelling music, slightly bitter-sweet. Philippe Abizanda is accompanied by drums, guitar and accordion, and honestly you could be nowhere else than passing joyously through the south of France when you hear it. We've got it on all the time now in our bistro back in Padstow, and David has commissioned Philippe to write some music for the television series mentioning lots of the local food on our journey. I can't wait to hear it.

Our second barge, the *Anjodi*, carried us all the way from Toulouse to Port St-Louis on the eastern bank of the mouth of the Rhône, which was the closest we could get to our final destination, Marseille. The crew had what I would describe as a love–hate relationship with us. Leigh, the skipper, was English but had spent most of his life in France; he was completely fluent in French but also had a gloriously uncompromisingly British accent. Philippe, second-in-command, was straight from central casting: arrogant and devilishly attractive to women, but with a remarkable understanding of idiomatic British humour. Then there was Louis the cook, who loved the food of Marseille, and Sonia, who cleaned the cabins, poor girl. She had a faintly

Oyster shacks at Château d'Oléron on the Ile d'Oléron

bemused attitude to us. We wanted to please her.

Altogether they found us a bit of a handful. We were not like the normal gin-and-tonic-at-six passengers. For a start, David made enormous demands on them, requiring us to be driven out into the countryside to meet cheesemakers and winemakers, and off to the airport at all hours to pick up or drop off English visitors. At one time that meant me. I had to go back to the staff party in Padstow and to see Chalky.

Some nights we would be drinking in a carefree way with the crew, while at other times they would be muttering conspiratorially about us. Well, at least, we thought they were, in the wheelhouse at the stern. I don't blame them. You see, we don't always behave well when we are filming. Sometimes, yes, we do drink too much, laughing euphorically about the English settlers in France, the 'no-we-live-heres', or the self-appointed 'King of the Ducks', the farmer who was absolutely pissed when we filmed his foie gras farm and

tried to control his volatile flock with a series of high-pitched squeaks. The birds paid not the slightest attention. Sometimes we'd have enormous rows – me and David, anyway – and there'd be shouting and swearing. I remember on one occasion saying to him, 'And another thing, we've got to stop all this eating. I'm getting far too fat. I saw the rushes of me talking to the King of the Ducks yesterday and I'm like the side of a house.' Other times there would be aggro about the snorers in our midst as yet

another of the boat crew endured a sleepless night. Was it Pete the soundman or Chris the cameraman? Bernard the second director or David? Certainly not Arezoo, our lovely assistant producer, or me. Well, if it was me, no one would mind, because being the 'talent' I had my own cabin. Always felt a bit guilty about that.

I know that the crew added immeasurably to the whole experience. I still keep in touch with them and I will certainly look them out when I go bargin' again.

When we finally got to Port St-Louis and headed out to sea, David asked me to jump in. I pointed out that as we were in a mighty current from the Rhône I might well disappear for ever. But I think we all knew we had had the most marvellous time. Then it was a short trip to Marseille and an exceptional bouillabaisse at a restaurant on La Corniche called L'Epuisette, with my chef friend Simon Hopkinson, and a little piece to the camera afterwards to say that in my opinion food was alive and extremely well in France.

My enduring memory of the trip is all the markets we visited: Cadillac, Toulouse, Narbonne, and above all Nérac, near Agen. The quality and range of food in them and the attention to detail is why I think France is still the best. A final image: a farmer in Cadillac market with a small table and 15 bunches of his own white asparagus. He sold them all in about 20 minutes, packed up and left.

Le Pont Canal d'Agen, which takes the Canal des Deux Mers across the Garonne

Soups and starters

Steamed mussels in a puréed soup made with the cooking liquor and some vegetables such as celeriac and leek is particularly successful, especially when there is a generous pinch of saffron included. I always like to add a few mussels in the shell along with the rest of the mussel meats to improve the finished look. It's important to get the texture of the soup right before adding them, which is why I pass it first through a normal sieve then through an even finer sieve, called a chinois. And finally I can't stress strongly enough to reheat the mussels with extreme caution. The longer they cook, the more they lose their flavour of the sea.

Cream of mussel soup with celeriac, thyme and saffron *Serves 4*

750 g small mussels, cleaned
4 tablespoons dry white wine
50 g butter
225 g peeled celeriac, chopped
125 g leek, cleaned and sliced

1 small garlic clove, chopped
Approximately 750 ml *Fish stock* (see page 208)
Good pinch saffron strands

180 g vine-ripened tomatoes, roughly chopped
4 tablespoons crème fraîche
Salt and freshly ground black pepper

Put the mussels and 2 tablespoons of the wine into a medium-sized pan. Place over a high heat and cook for 2–3 minutes or until the mussels have just opened. Tip them into a colander set over a bowl to collect the cooking juices. Leave to cool slightly then remove three-quarters of the meats from the shells, cover and set aside.

Melt the butter in the clean pan, add the celeriac, leek, garlic and remaining wine. Cover and leave to cook gently for 5 minutes.

Put all but the last tablespoon or two of the mussel liquor (which might be a bit gritty) into a large measuring jug and make up to 900 ml with the fish stock. Add to the pan of vegetables with the saffron and tomato, cover and simmer gently for 30 minutes.

Leave the soup to cool slightly, then blend until smooth. First pass through a sieve, then pass once more through a chinois into a clean pan, bring back to the boil and stir in the crème fraîche and some seasoning to taste.

Remove the pan from the heat and stir in the mussels to warm them through briefly, but don't allow them to cook any more than they already have. Ladle the soup into warmed soup plates, trying to distribute the mussels evenly, and serve straight away.

Previous page: The lighthouse at Brignogan, Brittany

It's a continuing disappointment to me that spider crabs are still not easy to get in the UK. This is not so in France, where I came up with this recipe, but for us I've had to suggest brown crab as an alternative. I'm not saying the brown crab makes an inferior soup, but there is something wonderfully fragrant and sweet about the meat of a spider crab. The whole point of this soup is to sum up the seafood flavours of Provence.

Spider crab soup
with fennel, tomato and Pernod *Serves 4–6*

1 x 500-g cooked spider or brown crab
1 leek
1 bulb fennel
1.2 litres vegetable stock
2 tomatoes (about 175 g), skinned
  and seeded

4 tablespoons olive oil
Small pinch crushed dried chillies
Pinch fennel seeds, lightly crushed
1 pared strip of orange peel
$^1/_2$ teaspoon tomato purée
4 garlic cloves, sliced

50 ml pastis, such as Pernod or
  Ricard
Juice $^1/_2$ orange
Pinch saffron strands
Salt and freshly ground black pepper

First, remove the white meat from the crab. Place the crab, back-shell down, on a chopping board and lift up, break off and discard the tail flap. Twist off all the legs, break them at the joints and discard all but the first, largest joints. Crack the shells of the legs with the back of a knife or a hammer and hook out the white meat with a crab pick. To remove the white meat from the body section, insert the blade of a large knife between the body and the back shell and twist to release it. Remove and reserve about 1 tablespoon of the brown meat from the back shell and discard the rest. Pull off the feathery looking gills or 'dead man's fingers' from the body and discard. Using a large knife, cut the body section into 4 and pick out the white meat from the little channels with a crab pick.

Clean and trim the leek and fennel. To make a stock, put the pieces of crab shell, the leek and fennel trimmings, the tablespoon of brown meat and the vegetable stock into a large pan, bring slowly up to the boil, skimming off any scum as it rises to the surface, cover and simmer for 30 minutes.

Meanwhile, cut the leek lengthways into quarters, then across into pieces the size of a small fingernail. Cut the fennel and seeded tomato into similar-sized pieces.

Warm the olive oil in another pan, add the dried chilli, fennel seeds, orange peel, tomato purée, garlic, leek and fennel and cook gently for 5 minutes without letting it colour. Increase the heat a little, add the pastis and light it with a match to burn off the alcohol. Strain over the stock through a fine sieve, add the orange juice and saffron and simmer for 10 minutes.

Now add the crabmeat and tomato and season to taste with salt and pepper. Ladle into warmed soup plates and serve straight away.

I first tasted this classic garlic soup at a ferme d'auberge near Marmande. Interesting that in France, to supplement their income at a time of difficulty in agriculture, some farmers are opening little restaurants on their farms. It was charming. I sat there in solitary splendour with the sounds of goats, chickens and ducks all around, and the first course was this rather delicate soup with threads of egg white in it, almost Chinese in appearance.

Tourin d'ail

Gascon garlic soup *Serves 4*

2 x 40-g heads garlic

2 tablespoons goose or duck fat

1 medium onion, peeled and
   chopped

20 g plain flour

1.2 litres *Chicken stock* (see page 208)

2 eggs, separated

1 teaspoon white wine vinegar

4 slices pain de campagne (rustic
   white bread), halved

Salt and freshly ground black pepper

1 tablespoon chopped parsley, to
   garnish

Remove the outer papery layer of skin from the heads of garlic. Cut each one horizontally in half and break the cloves away from the hard, woody core, but there's no need to peel them.

Melt the duck fat in a medium-sized pan. Add the onion and garlic and cook over a medium heat for 10 minutes, stirring now and then, until soft and very lightly browned.

Stir in the flour, then gradually add the stock and bring to the boil, stirring. Add 1 teaspoon of salt and 6 turns of the black pepper mill, cover and leave to simmer gently for 30 minutes.

Leave the soup to cool a little, then liquidize until smooth and pass through a sieve (to remove the garlic skins) back into a clean pan.

Whip the egg whites lightly with a fork until slightly frothy. Mix the egg yolks with the vinegar. Bring the soup back to the boil, adjust the seasoning if necessary, then remove from the heat and trickle the egg whites slowly into the soup, stirring all the time, so that they form long thin strands. Add 3 tablespoons of the hot soup to the egg yolks and stir back into the soup, but do not reheat or they will curdle and make the soup granular.

Toast the slices of bread over a naked flame. Put 2 pieces of bread into the bottom of 4 warmed soup plates and ladle over the soup. Sprinkle with a little chopped parsley and serve straight away.

Why yet another recipe for French onion soup, you may ask? The simple answer is that I have an enthusiasm for rescuing previously special recipes that have become too popular and thus subject to corner-cutting or over-inventiveness. The main constituents of a good onion soup to me are onions – lots of them – slowly cooked over a long period to make them sweet, caramel brown and soft, a good beef stock, and Gruyère cheese, which must be served bubbling and aromatic on top of the whole soup.

French onion soup *Serves 4*

60 g butter
1 kg onions, halved and thinly sliced
4 garlic cloves, finely chopped
2 teaspoons caster sugar
300 ml dry white wine

1.5 litres *Beef stock*, browned (see page 208)
Bouquet garni of bay leaves, thyme and parsley stalks
4 x 2.5-cm-thick slices French bread

225 g Gruyère or Comté cheese, coarsely grated
Salt and freshly ground black pepper

Heat the butter in a large, heavy-based pan. Add the onions, garlic and sugar and cook over a medium heat, stirring regularly, for 20–30 minutes until the onions are really soft and well caramelized.

Add the wine and leave to simmer rapidly until it has reduced by half.

Add the beef stock and bouquet garni, cover and leave the soup to simmer for at least another 30 minutes. Then remove and discard the bouquet garni, and season the soup to taste with salt and pepper.

Meanwhile, preheat the oven to 150°C/Gas Mark 2. Place the slices of bread onto a baking tray and leave them for 30 minutes to dry out but not get at all brown. Then remove the tray and increase the oven temperature to 220°C/Gas Mark 7.

To serve, place a slice of bread into the bottom of each of 4 deep ovenproof soup bowls and ladle the soup on top, making sure the onions and stock are distributed evenly. Cover the top of the soup thickly with the grated cheese, place the bowls onto a sturdy baking tray and bake for 30 minutes until golden and bubbling. You can also place them under a hot grill for 5 minutes if you prefer or are short of time. This soup should be served scalding hot.

Much as I love spinach soup, to make it an attractive recipe there needs to be a little extra going on. In this case the soup is faintly flavoured with nutmeg and finished with a poached egg and lots of freshly grated Parmesan. I based the flavours on a favourite dish of mine, Oeufs Florentine.

Deep green spinach soup
with a poached egg and Parmesan *Serves 6*

50 g butter
1 large onion, finely chopped
1 leek, cleaned, trimmed and thinly
  sliced
2 sticks celery, chopped

25 g plain flour
1.2 litres *Chicken stock* (see page 208)
500 g young leaf spinach, washed
Freshly grated nutmeg
6 large, very fresh eggs

White wine vinegar
Salt and freshly ground black pepper
50 g Parmesan cheese, finely grated,
  plus extra to serve

Melt the butter in a medium-sized pan. Add the onion, leek and celery, cover and cook gently for 10 minutes until soft but not browned.

Stir in the flour and cook gently for 1 minute. Then gradually add the stock and bring to the boil, stirring. Cover, lower the heat and leave to simmer for 30 minutes.

Stir the spinach into the hot soup and as soon as it has wilted down – this is to help keep its bright green colour – liquidize in batches until smooth. Return to a clean pan, season to taste with nutmeg, salt and pepper, but don't reheat just yet.

To poach the eggs, bring 5 cm of water to the boil in a wide, shallow pan. Add vinegar and salt (1$\frac{1}{2}$ teaspoons vinegar and $\frac{1}{2}$ teaspoon salt per 1.2 litres water) and reduce to a very gentle simmer. Break in the eggs and leave to poach gently for 3 minutes. Lift out with a slotted spoon and drain briefly on kitchen paper.

Reheat the soup, then ladle into warmed soup plates and slide a poached egg into the centre of each. Sprinkle over the Parmesan cheese and serve straight away, with a small bowl of extra Parmesan.

For this soup you need a sweet and firm pumpkin like the rouge vif d'Etampes, a French variety, sometimes also known as the Cinderella pumpkin because of its size and shape. All pumpkins are squashes and the soup can equally be made with varieties such as the kabocha or butternut, which have a sweet concentrated flavour that is further enhanced by roasting. I'm sure that a purist would make this soup with water instead of vegetable stock, but it's a frequent observation of pumpkins that in addition to having a good deal of natural sweetness they absorb and retain the flavour of whatever they are cooked with, and this recipe does seem to draw attention to a very good stock.

Roasted pumpkin and thyme soup

with Gruyère cheese *Serves 4*

1.5 kg unpeeled pumpkin, or
  kabocha or butternut squash
A little sunflower oil
40 g butter

1 medium onion, chopped
Leaves from 4 small sprigs of thyme,
  plus a few extra leaves to garnish
1.2 litres vegetable stock

150 ml single cream
75 g Gruyère cheese, coarsely grated
Salt and freshly ground black pepper

Preheat the oven to 200°C/Gas Mark 6. Cut the pumpkin or squash into chunky wedges and scoop away all the fibres and seeds. Rub them with oil, season well with salt and pepper and put them into a small roasting tin, skin-side down. Roast for 30 minutes until tender.

Remove the pumpkin from the oven and when cool enough to handle, slice away and discard the skin and cut the flesh into small chunks.

Melt the butter in a large pan, add the onion and half the thyme leaves and cook gently for about 10 minutes until the onion is very soft but not browned. Add the roasted pumpkin, any juices from the plate, the stock and ¹/₂ teaspoon of salt. Cover and simmer gently for 20 minutes.

Leave the soup to cool slightly, then blend with the rest of the thyme leaves until smooth. Return to a clean pan and bring back to a gentle simmer. Stir in the cream and adjust the seasoning if necessary. Ladle into warmed bowls and pile the grated Gruyère into the centre. Scatter with a few more thyme leaves and serve.

This is a typically clear, light, Vietnamese-style soup with noodles, dumplings and some thinly sliced salad vegetables, which are warmed in the soup just prior to serving rather than cooked through.

Prawn dumpling and noodle soup
with chilli, mint and coriander *Serves 4*

FOR THE SOUP:
The ingredients for 2 quantities of
   Chicken stock (see page 208)
8 garlic cloves, sliced
5-cm piece ginger, peeled and sliced
3 tablespoons Thai fish sauce
160 g thin Asian-style noodles,
   soaked if necessary

1 medium-hot red chilli, thinly sliced
4 teaspoons lime juice
30 g spring onions, trimmed and
   very thinly sliced on the diagonal
120 g fresh beansprouts
5 g small mint leaves
5 g coriander leaves

FOR THE DUMPLINGS:
240 g lean minced pork
2-g pinch Thai shrimp paste
   (blachan)
1 medium egg
80 g peeled raw prawns
Salt

Put the stock ingredients in a saucepan, add the garlic, ginger and fish sauce, and leave to simmer for 1 hour. Strain into a clean pan and continue to simmer until reduced to 1.2 litres. Keep hot.

To make the dumplings, put the minced pork into a food processor with the shrimp paste, egg and $1/4$ teaspoon salt and process into a smooth paste. Slice the prawns lengthways, remove the black, threadlike vein, and then slice them across into small pieces. Transfer the minced pork paste to a bowl and stir in the chopped prawns. Shape 10–15-g pieces of the mixture into small balls and place on an opened-out petal steamer.

Heat the 4 deep soup bowls in a low oven. Fill a large shallow pan with water to a depth of 2 cm and bring to the boil. Add the petal steamer of dumplings, reduce the heat to a simmer, cover and steam for 4 minutes, or until cooked through.

Divide the noodles, chilli, lime juice, spring onions, beansprouts, mint and coriander leaves between the heated bowls and top with the dumplings. Bring the stock back to the boil, pour into each bowl and serve straight away.

I have very fond memories of this soup from the Great Western Hotel in Paddington where I was a commis chef in the sixties. When vichyssoise was ordered, a tin was produced from the stores, opened with great gravity and the contents transferred to a tureen set in ice. The tin came from France and in those days it was assumed that the contents would be better than anything we could make ourselves. Well, of course, that wasn't the case, and this recipe is an absolute winner. Vichyssoise is far and away my favourite chilled soup.

Vichyssoise *Serves 6*

1 kg leeks, cleaned
50 g butter
225 g onion, chopped
225 g peeled floury potatoes, sliced

900 ml *Chicken stock* (see page 208)
150 ml double cream
200 ml full-cream milk
1 small bunch chives, finely chopped

Salt and freshly ground white pepper

You only want the white part of the leeks for this soup, so cut them into two, where they start to change colour, and very thinly slice the white part. You need to be left with 500 g. Melt the butter in a large pan, add the leek, onion and potatoes and cook over a gentle heat for 10 minutes until very soft but not coloured.

Add the stock, 1 teaspoon of salt and some white pepper. Bring to a gentle simmer, cover and cook for 30 minutes.

Leave to cool slightly, then blend the soup in a liquidizer or food processor until smooth. Pass through a fine sieve into a clean pan and leave to cool, then stir in the cream and the milk. Adjust the seasoning to taste, cover and chill for at least a few hours, or overnight.

Ladle the soup into chilled soup plates and serve sprinkled with the chopped chives.

Onion fields, Castelnaudary

*I can't understand why sorrel isn't more popular.
It grows everywhere in hedgerows, but it is still
relatively difficult to get in the supermarket. Yet
a handful of thinly sliced leaves, thrown into this
soup at the last minute, gives what is already a
lovely soup a fresh tartness.*

Sorrel, pea and lettuce soup *Serves 4*

50 g butter

**2 bunches spring onions, trimmed
  and thinly sliced**

**4 little gem hearts, shredded,
  washed and dried in a salad spinner**

450 g fresh or frozen petit pois

1.2 litres *Chicken stock* (see page 208)

25 g sorrel leaves

**50 ml single cream, plus a little extra
  to serve**

Salt and freshly ground white pepper

Melt the butter in a large pan, add the spring onions and cook gently for 3–4 minutes until soft but without letting them colour. Add the lettuce and cook gently for 2 minutes. Add the peas and cook for a further 2 minutes. Add the stock, 1½ teaspoons salt and a little white pepper, bring to the boil, cover and leave to simmer for just 5 minutes.

Leave the soup to cool slightly, then blend until smooth and pass through a sieve into a clean pan. Bring back to a gentle simmer and adjust the seasoning if necessary.

Bunch up the sorrel leaves and cut them across into very fine strips. Stir into the soup with the cream and leave to cook for 1 minute. Ladle into warm soup bowls and serve garnished with an extra swirl of single cream.

Bernard, the skipper of the first barge on the trip from Bordeaux to Marseilles, used to make a melon salad as a first course while we were passing through the vast fruit-growing area around Agen. This salad is in memory of a trip to Quercy, and a day spent with the Dussac family on their melon farm. We were enchanted by the grandparents, who had been married for 54 years. I asked them what the secret of their long and clearly delighted marriage was, and he pointed his finger upwards. The crew predictably thought he was pointing to the bedroom. I, probably because I'm a cook, assumed he was pointing towards the abundant sun in that part of France. He was, in fact, pointing towards God.

Charentais melon salad
with tomato, cucumber and goat's cheese *Serves 4*

$^1/_2$ **ripe, orange-fleshed melon, such
  as Charentais or Canteloupe**
$^1/_2$ **cucumber**
**225 g vine-ripened tomatoes,
  skinned**
**100 g firm, crumbly goat's cheese,
  such as Chevrissime Blanc**
1 tablespoon finely shredded mint

FOR THE DRESSING:
3 tablespoons olive oil
1 tablespoon red wine vinegar
Pinch caster sugar
**Sea salt flakes and coarsely ground
  black pepper**

For the salad dressing, whisk the oil, vinegar and sugar together with some sea salt flakes and pepper to taste. Set to one side.

Cut the melon into four wedges and scoop out the seeds with a spoon. Slice the flesh neatly away from the skin and then slice each wedge diagonally into long thin slices.

Peel the cucumber and slice on the diagonal into 3-mm-thick slices. Slice the tomatoes.

Arrange the sliced melon over the base of a large serving plate and cover with the sliced cucumber and tomatoes. Crumble the goat's cheese into small pieces over the top of the salad, and then scatter over the mint. Spoon over the dressing and serve straight away.

The TV crew and I were taken aback by this dish at a restaurant at Le Sambuc in the Camargue. There's nothing much to it, really. It's a selection of crudités served with a pungent anchovy sauce made from local salted anchovies, but you couldn't think of a more vibrant expression through food of the life in that part of southern France. I think that's what is so special about the cooking there. Like Italy, it's all about using few, simple ingredients...

L'anchoïade with crudités *Serves 4–6*

FOR THE ANCHOÏADE:
1 x 50 g tin anchovy fillets in olive oil
1 garlic clove, roughly chopped
¹/₂ teaspoon red wine vinegar
150 ml extra virgin olive oil
Freshly ground black pepper

FOR THE CRUDITÉS:
1 large bunch radishes
1 bulb fennel
225 g cauliflower
225 g small new potatoes, scrubbed clean
125 g fine green beans, trimmed

First prepare the vegetables. Trim the radishes of most of their leaves and wash thoroughly. Trim the fennel and cut it lengthways through the root into very thin slices, so that they stay together in one piece. Break the cauliflower into small, bite-sized florets. Put the potatoes into a pan of well-salted cold water, bring to the boil and cook for 12–15 minutes or until just tender. Bring another pan of well-salted water to boil for the beans.

Meanwhile, make the anchoïade. If you like it smooth, put the anchovies, garlic and 20 turns of the black pepper mill into a food processor and blend to a paste. Add the red wine vinegar and blend briefly, then, with the machine still running, gradually add the olive oil in a slow and steady stream to make a smooth, emulsified sauce. If you prefer it a little chunkier, pound the anchovies and their oil, the garlic and black pepper together in a mortar with a pestle, then gradually add the vinegar and oil. Transfer the mixture to a small, shallow serving bowl.

Drain the potatoes and leave them to cool slightly. Meanwhile, drop the beans into the other pan of boiling water and cook for 3–4 minutes until just cooked but still with a little bite to them. Drain and refresh briefly under running cold water, but not for too long because you want them to be slightly warm.

Arrange the vegetables on a large serving platter and take to the table with the bowl of anchoïade and some plates. The idea is that people help themselves to the vegetables and drizzle them with as much of the anchoïade as they like.

I've always loved brandade – a thick purée of salt cod, garlic, olive oil and cream – but it was our executive chef Roy Brett who came up with this way of serving it. He looks after all the kitchens in Padstow while I'm off making TV programmes, writing cookery books and travelling the world for new ideas. He puts it in a small, oval gratin dish, covers it with a layer of breadcrumbs and browns it under the grill. He then adds some fingers of toast dipped in tapenade: a paste of olives and anchovy. You'd have thought that adding one salt fish to another would be too much, but actually the pungent flavour of anchovy emphasized by black olives is very satisfying. I've written a method for making your own salt cod, though when I cooked this on the barge, the Rosa, *on the canal, the* Latéral à la Garonne, *I used salt cod we bought from an artisanal factory outside Bordeaux.*

Brandade de morue with anchovy toasts *Serves 6*

450 g *Fresh salted cod* (see page 210)
3 garlic cloves, crushed
120 ml olive oil
175 ml double cream
6 heaped teaspoons coarse white breadcrumbs or Japanese panko crumbs
Lemon juice, salt and freshly ground black pepper to taste

FOR THE ANCHOVY TOASTS:
6 slices medium-thick white bread, crusts removed
40 g *Clarified butter* (see page 210)
3 tablespoons *Tapenade* (see page 74)

FOR THE SALAD GARNISH:
1 teaspoon freshly squeezed lemon juice
3 teaspoons extra virgin olive oil
50 g prepared salad frisée

Cover the salt cod with plenty of fresh cold water and leave it to soak for 1 hour. Meanwhile, for the anchovy toasts, cut each slice of bread into 3 fingers. Fry in the clarified butter for a minute or two on either side until golden brown. Drain briefly on kitchen paper and keep warm in a low oven. Whisk together the lemon juice, olive oil and salt and pepper for the salad garnish and set to one side.

For the brandade, drain the soaked salted cod and remove the skin and any bones. Put it into a pan with enough fresh water to cover, bring to the boil and simmer for 5 minutes. Lift out with a slotted spoon, drain away the excess water and then put into a food processor.

Put the garlic, olive oil and cream into a small pan and bring to the boil. Add to the fish in the processor and blend together until just smooth. Season to taste with lemon juice and plenty of black pepper, but only add salt if necessary.

Preheat the grill to high. Spoon the mixture into 6 deep oval ramekins and smooth off the surface with a palette knife. Scatter the top of each one with a heaped teaspoon of the breadcrumbs, grill for about 20 seconds until the crumbs are crisp and golden brown, then transfer the dishes to 6 serving plates. Spoon ¹/₂ teaspoon of the tapenade onto one end of each toast and arrange 3 on each plate. Toss the salad frisée with the dressing, pile alongside the toasts, and serve.

Lightly curried crab mayonnaise
with lamb's lettuce *Serves 4*

3–4 medium-sized vine-ripened tomatoes

5 tablespoons *Mayonnaise* (see page 209)

¹/₂ teaspoon mild curry powder

¹/₂ teaspoon lemon juice

2 dashes Tabasco sauce

500 g fresh white crabmeat

50 g lamb's lettuce, roots trimmed

2 teaspoons extra virgin olive oil

Salt

Fresh wholemeal bread, to serve

Skin the tomatoes by plunging them into boiling water for about 20 seconds. As soon as the skins split, remove and cover with cold water to stop them cooking any further. Peel off the skins and cut each tomato into very thin slices, discarding the top and bottom.

Put the mayonnaise into a bowl and stir in the curry powder, lemon juice and Tabasco sauce. Fold this mixture lightly through the crabmeat and season to taste with a little salt.

Overlap a few slices of tomato into the centre of 4 small plates and season them lightly with salt. Spoon some of the crab mayonnaise on top. Toss the lamb's lettuce with the olive oil and a small pinch of salt and pile alongside. Serve with some wholemeal bread.

The lighthouse at St Mathieu, Brittany

I just had to put sauce mignonette with oysters from one of the étangs – the saltwater lagoons just behind the Mediterranean that are separated from the sea by a spit of sand between Perpignan and Marseilles. The first time I ever ate oysters was here, at Port St Louis, served with this flavoured vinegar. It seems to work particularly well with these oysters, which have a high saline content. The locals rate fish caught from the étangs higher than those caught in the Mediterranean itself. They attribute the superior flavour to more salt in the water.

Oysters with sauce mignonette *Serves 2*

1 dozen oysters

FOR THE SAUCE MIGNONETTE:
3 tablespoons good quality white wine
   vinegar

1 teaspoon sunflower oil
$^1/_4$ teaspoon coarsely crushed white
   peppercorns
1 tablespoon very thinly sliced spring
   onion tops

To open the oysters, wrap one hand in a tea towel and hold the oyster in it with the flat shell uppermost. Push the point of an oyster knife into the hinge, located at the narrowest point, and wiggle the knife back and forth until the hinge breaks and you can slide the knife between the two shells. Twist the point of the knife upwards to lever up the top shell, cut through the ligament and lift off the top shell. Release the oyster meat from the bottom shell and remove, picking out any little bits of shell.

    Mix together the ingredients for the sauce just before serving. Arrange the oysters on plates, spoon a little of the sauce onto each one and serve.

Oyster beds, Etang-de-Thau

I dreamt up this escabèche after a visit to the Salins du Midi just outside Aigues-Mortes, a fascinating succession of sea-salt pans, the total acreage covered greater than that of Paris. As the water evaporates under the hot Mediterranean sun, the algae in the water, which is normally green, die and turn the water a delicate shade of pink, which is also the colour of the flamingos flying overhead. It was a memorable colour scheme: blue early morning sky, dazzling piles of white salt, pink water and birds. And the salt, fleur de sel, is definitely more interesting in flavour than bog-standard table salt. It lasts longer in the mouth, and it has inspired this escabèche, using the abundant fennel stalks that grow everywhere there and Mediterranean mackerel.

Mackerel escabèche
with oregano, fennel and chilli *Serves 4*

2 mackerel, about 300–350 g each, filleted
15 g plain flour
25 g thick, fleshy, fennel herb stalks
4 spring onions

1 medium-hot red chilli, stalk removed
80 ml extra virgin olive oil
80 ml white wine vinegar
5 sprigs of oregano, thyme or rosemary

Fleur de sel or sea salt and freshly ground black pepper
Cold Rosé de Provence wine and pain rustique (rustic white bread), to serve

Slice the fish, slightly on the diagonal, into pieces 2.5 cm wide and toss with a little salt and then the flour. Slice the fennel stalks, spring onions and red chilli slightly on the diagonal too.

Heat a large frying pan over a high heat, add half the oil and fry the mackerel pieces for 3 minutes, turning them over halfway through. Transfer to a shallow serving dish.

Add the vinegar to the frying pan and boil rapidly until reduced by two-thirds. Add 100 ml water and another ¹/₂ teaspoon of salt and the vegetables, oregano, thyme or rosemary, the rest of the olive oil and 20 turns of black pepper. Boil once more until reduced by half.

Pour the mixture over the fish and leave to go cold, turning the fish 2 or 3 times as it cools, but don't refrigerate it. This is far better served at room temperature. Transfer to a flat, oval platter, and serve on the poop deck with a cold Rosé de Provence and some slices of pain rustique.

I actually think there are few accompaniments to a drinks party that really work. Maybe goujons of lemon sole with homemade tartare sauce, Thai fish cakes and a sweet chilli dipping sauce, quail's eggs and celery salt ... but hard to beat would be gougères, recently baked, made using Gruyère cheese, with their soft, cheesy centres, crisp exterior and light-as-a-feather texture.

Gougères

Makes approximately 30

75 g butter
215 ml cold water
95 g plain flour, sifted

3 large eggs, beaten
75 g finely grated Gruyère cheese
Salt

Preheat the oven to 200°C/Gas Mark 6. Put the butter and water into a pan and leave over a low heat until the butter has melted. Meanwhile, sift together the flour and ¼ teaspoon of salt. When the butter has melted, turn up the heat, bring the mixture to the boil and add the flour. Beat vigorously until the mixture is smooth and leaves the sides of the pan, then leave to cool slightly before gradually beating in the eggs to make a smooth, glossy choux paste. Beat in three-quarters of the cheese.

Drop heaped teaspoons of the mixture, about 3–4 cm apart, onto a large, well-greased baking sheet. Sprinkle with the rest of the cheese and bake for 20–25 minutes until puffed up, crisp and golden. Serve warm, with a glass of lightly chilled Beaujolais.

This looks very easy, and indeed it is, but it requires serious attention to detail. It's a perfect example of why a recipe doesn't tell the whole story – so here are a few points to consider. The mussels must be perfectly fresh and tightly closed. They should be cooked for the briefest possible time, and removed from the source of heat when the meats have plumped up and the shells just opened. The salad should be made while the mussels are still warm. The waxy potatoes should also be freshly cooked, perhaps with a little mint, and served still warm. The salad leaves should be crisp and fresh, and the pistou freshly made with good olive oil and perfumed basil. Finally, the salad should be put together with a deftness of touch so that it looks like the picture opposite. No pressure here then! The recipe for the pistou makes a bit too much for this recipe, but it's difficult to make in smaller amounts. Store it in a screw-top jar in the fridge and use within 2 to 3 days; it's great stirred into vegetable soups or pasta.

Warm mussel and potato salad with pistou

Serves 4

350 g small waxy potatoes, such as
  rattes, pink fir apple or Anya
750 g medium-sized mussels
50 g prepared frisée (curly endive)
50 g wild rocket
¼ lemon, for squeezing

FOR THE PISTOU:
50 g fresh basil leaves
3 fat garlic cloves, peeled
1 x 75 g vine-ripened tomato,
  skinned, seeded and chopped
75 g Parmesan cheese, finely grated

150 ml olive oil
Salt and freshly ground black pepper

Peel the potatoes and put them into a pan of cold salted water (1 teaspoon per 600 ml). Bring to the boil and cook for 12–15 minutes until tender. Drain, return to the pan, cover and keep warm.

For the pistou, put the basil, garlic, tomato and Parmesan cheese into a food processor and blend. Then, with the machine still running, gradually add the oil to make a mayonnaise-like mixture. Season to taste with ¼ teaspoon of salt and some black pepper.

Put the mussels and 2 tablespoons of water into a medium-sized pan, cover and place over a high heat. Cook for 2–3 minutes, shaking the pan once or twice, until the mussels have just opened. Tip into a colander set over a bowl to collect the juices, and when they are cool enough to handle, remove all but a few of them from the shells. Cover and keep warm. Return the mussel-cooking liquor to the pan and boil rapidly until reduced and well flavoured.

Put 4 tablespoons of the pistou into a small bowl and stir in 2 teaspoons of the reduced mussel cooking liquor to loosen it slightly.

Mix the frisée with the rocket and divide between 4 plates. Slice the potatoes and arrange them in among the leaves with the mussels. Drizzle over the pistou, squeeze over a little lemon juice and serve straight away, while the potatoes are still warm.

Everybody loves seared scallops. The problem is that in many restaurants they are partnered with things that leave you wondering why: large lumps of black pudding, potato choux balls, ponzu sauce, you-name-it. Here I've just used a well-reduced tomato dressing with good olive oil, and added a pile of cooked lentils and a squeeze of lemon.

Seared scallops with lentils
and a tomato and herbes de Provence dressing *Serves 4*

100 g Puy lentils
2¹/₂ tablespoons olive oil
12–16 large prepared scallops
Salt and freshly ground black pepper

FOR THE DRESSING:
7 tablespoons extra virgin olive oil
4 small garlic cloves, finely chopped
4 medium-sized vine tomatoes,
   skinned, seeded and chopped
¹/₂ teaspoon chopped mixed
   rosemary and thyme or large pinch
   dried herbes de Provence

2 tablespoons red wine vinegar
1 teaspoon caster sugar
1 tablespoon freshly squeezed lemon
   juice
1 teaspoon mixed chopped parsley
   and basil

For the dressing, put 2 tablespoons of the extra virgin olive oil and the garlic into a small pan, and place over a medium-high heat. As soon as the garlic begins to sizzle, add the tomatoes and chopped rosemary and thyme, or herbes de Provence, and simmer for 10–12 minutes until well reduced and thick. Put the vinegar and sugar into another small pan and boil rapidly until reduced to 2 teaspoons. Stir into the tomato sauce, season to taste with some salt and pepper and set to one side.

Bring a pan of well-salted water to the boil (1 teaspoon per 600 ml). Add the lentils and cook for 15–20 minutes or until tender. Drain well, return to the pan with ¹/₂ tablespoon of the olive oil and some salt and pepper, cover and keep warm.

Slice each scallop horizontally into 2 thinner discs, leaving the roe attached to one slice. Place in a shallow dish with the remaining 2 tablespoons of olive oil and some salt and pepper and toss together well.

To finish the tomato dressing, add the remaining 5 tablespoons of extra virgin olive oil, the lemon juice and some salt to taste and leave to heat through gently over a very low heat. Meanwhile, heat a dry, reliably non-stick frying pan over a high heat until smoking hot. Lower the heat slightly, add 1 teaspoon of oil and half the scallop slices and sear them for 1 minute on each side until golden brown. Lift onto a plate and repeat with the rest.

Divide the lentils between 4 warmed plates and arrange the scallop slices alongside. Stir the chopped basil and parsley into the warm tomato dressing, spoon some over and around the scallops and serve straight away.

There's only one way of buying duck foie gras — you have to get a whole raw liver, weighing about 700–800 g, so I've written a recipe for 8 or 10 people, which is probably only for high days and holidays. The business of pan-frying foie gras tends to make people panic, but don't worry. The method below gives a deliciously caramelized exterior and a soft and slightly underdone centre. I think this recipe originally came from Rowley Leigh and it's ever so good, particularly when served with the deglaze made at the end with port, chicken stock and balsamic vinegar.

Seared foie gras on sweetcorn pancakes
with a balsamic vinegar and port glaze *Serves 8–10*

1 whole duck foie gras, weighing
  about 700–800 g
Salt and freshly ground black pepper

FOR THE SWEETCORN PANCAKES:
90 g mashed potato
115 g plain flour

¹/₄ teaspoon baking powder
2 medium eggs
170 ml milk
¹/₂ teaspoon salt
1 x 198 g can sweetcorn kernels,
  drained
60 ml sunflower oil, for shallow frying

FOR THE PORT GLAZE:
150 ml ruby port
150 ml *Chicken stock* (see page 208),
  or water
1 tablespoon good balsamic vinegar
1¹/₂ teaspoons *Beurre manié* (see
  page 210)

Cut the foie gras across into 1-cm-thick slices. They might fall apart a little but don't worry. Put them back in the fridge so they remain very cold while you make the pancakes.

Make a batter with the mashed potato, flour, baking powder, eggs, milk and salt. You will probably have to pass it through a sieve to get rid of any potato lumps. Stir in the drained sweetcorn kernels.

You need to make neat round pancakes 9 cm in diameter, so either use a blini pan, or plain pastry cutters inside an ordinary frying pan. You can get 4 pastry cutters into a standard 28–30-cm frying pan. Heat the oil in the pan, add the oiled rings and pour 35–40 g batter into each ring. Cook over a medium heat for 2 minutes, then remove the cutters, flip over the pancakes and cook for 2 minutes on the other side. Remove, drain on kitchen paper and keep warm in a low oven while you cook the rest.

To cook the foie gras, heat a dry, non-stick frying pan over a high heat until very hot. Lower the heat slightly, add a few slices of the foie gras and cook for 30 seconds. Then turn them over, remove the pan from the heat and leave for 1 minute 15 seconds. Carefully remove the slices from the pan to a plate and leave in a warm place (but not the oven). Pour away all the fat from the pan into a bowl (but keep it, as it's a very good frying medium for bread with a cooked breakfast), wipe out with kitchen paper and repeat with the remaining slices. After the last batch of foie gras is cooked, pour away the excess fat from the pan, return it to a high heat and add the port, chicken stock and balsamic vinegar. Boil rapidly until reduced by half and then whisk in the beurre manié and a little seasoning to taste.

Put one pancake onto each warmed plate and top with slices of the seared foie gras. Spoon a tablespoon of the glaze around the outside of the plate and serve straight away.

This is based on a recipe for jambon persillé *but using ham hocks rather than leg. It took quite a lot of testing to get it just right. What I was looking for was the right ratio of meat to parsley jelly, and trying to give the correct tartness to the jelly by the careful addition of a little cider vinegar. I've also wrapped the terrine in blanched Savoy cabbage leaves, since it's intended for service in our bistro and looks really nice when sliced, but feel free to line the dish with clingfilm instead. You need to be a bit choosy about ham hocks. Buy from a butcher with a good reputation for pork and ham. It will make all the difference to the finished flavour of the terrine.*

Ham hock terrine
with a chicory and mustard salad *Serves 8–10*

4 x 1.2-kg ham hocks
2 onions, peeled and thickly sliced
450 g carrots, peeled and thickly sliced
3 celery sticks, sliced
2 large sprigs of thyme
2 bay leaves
Large bunch curly parsley, divided
  into stalks and leaves

6 cloves
10 black peppercorns
65 ml cider vinegar
1 x 5-g sheet of leaf gelatine
1 large Savoy cabbage
Salt and freshly ground black pepper

FOR THE CHICORY AND MUSTARD
SALAD:
6–8 small heads chicory
2 teaspoons Dijon mustard
2 teaspoons white wine vinegar
10 teaspoons extra virgin olive oil
1$^1/_2$ teaspoons *Persillade* (see page
  210)

The first thing to do is ascertain how salty your ham hocks are. This will depend on the supplier and the cure. Take a thin slice off one hock, drop it into a pan of simmering water and leave it to cook for a few minutes. Taste it, and if at all salty, then put the hocks into a large pan, cover with plenty of cold water and leave to soak overnight.

The next day, drain the ham hocks, put them back into the pan and cover with fresh cold water. Bring to the boil, skimming off the scum as it rises to the surface, and add the onions, carrots, celery, thyme, bay leaves, parsley stalks, cloves, peppercorns and vinegar. Cover and leave to simmer for 3 hours or until the bone from the centre of each hock will pull out easily.

Lift the hocks out of the liquid into a bowl and leave until cool enough to handle. Cover the bowl with some clingfilm to prevent the outside of the meat becoming dry.

Meanwhile, make the jelly. Taste the cooking liquor and if well flavoured, strain 600 ml through a fine sieve into a jug. If it tastes a little too salty, take less than 600 ml and dilute to taste with hot water; if it tastes a little watery, strain 1 litre into a pan and boil rapidly until slightly concentrated, then measure out the required amount. Now drop the sheet of leaf gelatine into a bowl of tepid water, and as soon as it has softened, lift it out, add to the hot stock and stir until dissolved. Leave to cool slightly.

Break off and discard any damaged outer leaves from the cabbage, then break away about another 6 prime, well-coloured leaves. Bring a large pan of well-salted water to the

boil, add the leaves and cook for about 3 minutes until just tender. Drain and refresh under running cold water, then drain once more and dry off on a clean tea towel. Slightly flatten the thick stem with a rolling pin. Lightly oil a 1.2-litre terrine dish or loaf tin (one measuring about 25 x 8 x 7 cm) and line with the cabbage leaves so that each one lies partly over the next one, with enough leaf overhanging to cover the base of the finished terrine.

While still warm, pull the meat off the hocks, leaving the pieces quite chunky, and discard all the skin, fat, bones and any tough sinew. Chop the parsley leaves; you need 50 g altogether. Put the meat into a bowl with 25 g of the chopped parsley and mix together well. Mix another 15 g of the parsley into the jelly mixture. Pack a layer of ham pieces into the base of the terrine, sprinkle with a little of the remaining parsley and then pour over some of the jelly mixture to barely cover. Continue layering the meat, parsley and jelly like this until the terrine is full and everything has been used up. Fold over the edges of the cabbage leaves, then cover the surface of the terrine with a piece of foil-covered cardboard, cut to fit neatly inside the rim. Weight down with unopened cans or weights from measuring scales and leave to chill for at least 24 hours.

Shortly before serving, make the chicory salad. Trim the bases, break the chicory into separate leaves and put into a bowl. For the dressing, whisk the mustard and vinegar together, then gradually whisk in the oil and season to taste with salt and pepper. Toss the dressing with the chicory leaves, then sprinkle over the persillade and toss once more.

To serve, dip the terrine dish very briefly into a bowl of hot water and invert it onto a board. Carefully cut it across into 8–10-mm thick slices, overlap 2 slices onto each plate and pile some of the chicory salad alongside.

If you can, get hold of the sourdough bread called Poilâne. When grilled over an open flame, it is the perfect base for these calf's brains – I do think good bread is what makes this dish. This recipe is a classic French treatment for a very underrated form of offal. We serve this all the time on the menu of St Petroc's, our bistro in Padstow.

Sautéed calf's brains on toasted sourdough with beurre noisette *Serves 4*

2 calf's brains
50 g butter
4 teaspoons nonpareilles capers

FOR THE BEURRE NOISETTE:
100 g unsalted butter
1 tablespoon lemon juice
1½ heaped tablespoons chopped parsley

Salt and freshly ground black pepper

4 thin slices of sourdough bread, lightly toasted over a naked gas flame, to serve

Cover the calf's brains with cold water and leave them to soak for 24 hours, changing the water now and then, to rid them of any excess blood.

Bring 2.25 litres of water to the boil in a pan and add 1 tablespoon of salt. Split each brain into 2 lobes, drop them into the water, bring back to the boil and remove the pan from the heat. Leave them to cool in the liquid. They can be prepared in advance to this stage if you wish. Just chill in the fridge, in the liquid, until needed.

When you are ready to serve, take the brains from the liquid and remove pieces of membrane, any veins and so on. Slice each lobe lengthways into 3 or 4 slices.

Put a slice of toast onto each of 4 warmed plates and set to one side. Heat 25 g of the butter in a large frying pan, add half of the calf's brain slices and sear over a high heat for 1 minute on each side. Lift onto some of the toast slices and repeat with the rest of the butter and brains. Scatter with the capers.

For the beurre noisette, discard the frying oil from the pan and wipe it clean. Add the butter and allow it to melt over a moderate heat. As soon as it starts to smell nutty and turns light brown, add the lemon juice, parsley and some seasoning. Spoon over the brains and serve straight away.

This recipe is from Simon Hopkinson, who joined us for part of the filming while we were in Marseille. You might almost be asking yourself, do we really need a recipe for something so simple? Yet this is one of those classic dishes that has been forgotten, and yet is fantastic when well done, which is sadly not always the case.

Egg mayonnaise *Serves 6*

9 medium eggs
3 soft round lettuces

FOR THE MAYONNAISE:
2 egg yolks
1 tablespoon Dijon mustard

300 ml sunflower oil
100 ml light olive oil
Juice ¹/₂ lemon (about 1¹/₂ tablespoons)
1–2 tablespoons warm water
Salt and freshly ground white pepper

TO SERVE:
18 anchovy fillets in olive oil, drained
Cayenne pepper
Thinly sliced brown bread and butter

Put the eggs into a pan of cold water, bring to the boil and cook for 4 minutes. Refresh under running cold water for 3 minutes, then drain and peel. Cut them in half lengthways and lay them cut-side down on an oval serving dish.

Discard the outside, darker green leaves of the lettuces, break the hearts into separate leaves and wash and dry them well (in a salad spinner is ideal). Tuck the lettuce leaves around the edge of the eggs.

To make the mayonnaise, put the egg yolks, mustard, ¹/₂ teaspoon of salt and some white pepper into a bowl and beat with a wire whisk until thick. Gradually add the oils, whisking all the time, adding a little of the lemon juice every now and then, until the mixture is thick and glossy. Alternatively make it in a food processor (see page 209). Adjust the seasoning to taste and then whisk in the warm water so that the mayonnaise will coat the eggs in a silky smooth layer.

Cut the anchovy fillets in half and criss-cross them over the top of the eggs. Sprinkle lightly with cayenne pepper and serve with some thinly sliced brown bread and butter.

St Emilion

Bayonne ham with celeriac remoulade

Serves 6

1 large celeriac, weighing about 750 g
4 anchovy fillets in olive oil, drained
200 ml *Mayonnaise* (see page 209)

1 tablespoon Dijon mustard
18 x 10 g thin slices of Bayonne ham
1 tablespoon nonpareilles capers

For the celeriac remoulade, peel the celeriac, cut it into quarters and shred into long thin strands on a mandolin (or by hand). You should be left with 450–500 g. Put the anchovy fillets into a mortar and grind to a paste with the pestle, then stir in the mayonnaise and mustard. Stir into the celeriac and leave to marinate for 1 hour.

To serve, ruffle 3 slices of the ham on each plate and spoon some of the celeriac remoulade alongside. Scatter the capers over the celeriac and serve.

This is a Breton take on a classic salade composée, *done with soft round lettuce leaves and the addition of warm sliced artichoke hearts, which makes it the sort of local dish that will help you remember those fields of artichokes around St Pol de Leon, just near Morlaix. For me, getting off the ferry at Roscoff and driving past those green globes everywhere gives me a quiet thrill of having arrived back in lovely France, just as the smell of Gauloise used to.*

Poached eggs
with an artichoke, bacon and croûton salad *Serves 4*

4 large, very fresh eggs
White wine vinegar
Salt and freshly ground black pepper

FOR THE SALAD:
4 large globe artichokes
2 soft round lettuces
2 slices white bread, crusts removed
Sunflower oil, for shallow frying
4 rashers rindless, thick-cut streaky
   bacon, cut across into short fat strips

FOR THE DRESSING:
2 tablespoons white wine vinegar
$1/2$ teaspoon Dijon mustard
6 tablespoons sunflower oil

To prepare the artichokes, break off the stems and discard. Cut off the top half of each globe, and then bend back the green leaves, letting them snap off close to the base, until you reach the hairy choke at the centre. Slice the choke away with a small knife, close to the heart, or scrape it away with a teaspoon. Trim off the dark green base of the leaves to leave just the convex-shaped heart. Drop them into a pan of acidulated water (water and lemon juice) to prevent the hearts going brown. When you have prepared them all, bring a pan of salted water to the boil. Add the hearts and cook for 4–5 minutes or until just tender, then drain and leave to cool.

Remove the outer leaves of the lettuces and break the pale green hearts into leaves. Wash and dry well, using a salad spinner if you have one. Slice the artichoke hearts across into thin slices.

For the croûtons, tear or cut the bread into small pieces about 1 cm in size. Heat a thin layer of sunflower oil in a small frying pan, add the bread pieces and fry over a medium-high heat until crisp and golden. Remove with a slotted spoon and leave to drain on kitchen paper. Heat a little more sunflower oil in the frying pan, add the bacon strips and fry for 2–3 minutes until crisp. Set aside with the croûtons and keep warm.

To make the dressing, return the empty frying pan to a medium-high heat and add the vinegar, followed by the mustard. Whisk together well, allowing the mixture to reduce very slightly as you do so, then gradually whisk in the sunflower oil and some salt and pepper to taste. Turn off the heat and keep warm.

To poach the eggs, bring 5 cm of water to the boil in a wide, shallow pan. Add vinegar and salt (1½ teaspoons vinegar and ½ teaspoon salt per 1.2 litres water) and reduce to a very gentle simmer. Break in the eggs and leave to poach gently for 3 minutes. Lift out with a slotted spoon and drain briefly on kitchen paper.

To serve, arrange the salad leaves over the centre of 4 plates and tuck the artichoke slices in among the leaves. Slide a poached egg into the centre of each salad and scatter with the croûtons and bacon. Spoon over a little of the warm dressing and serve straight away, while everything is still warm.

Once upon a time, whole globe artichokes with vinaigrette were all the rage in bistros. It's a shame the dish has died out over here. The exciting thing about Bernard's (the skipper of the Rosa*) version is that having removed the choke, the hairy centre of the artichoke, he fills the dip with the dressing, then covers it with a little pink cone of the smaller leaves. It's those deft touches of presentation that I love so much about French food.*

Globe artichokes with mustard dressing

Serves 4

4 large globe artichokes
Salt and freshly ground black pepper

FOR THE MUSTARD DRESSING:
1 tablespoon Dijon mustard
2 tablespoons white wine vinegar
8 tablespoons light olive oil

Trim away the stems of each artichoke, so that they sit flat, then drop them into a large pan of boiling well-salted water (1 teaspoon per 600 ml) and keep submerged under a colander or heatproof bowl. Cook for 30–40 minutes until one of the leaves pulls away easily.

Meanwhile, whisk the mustard and vinegar together in a bowl and then gradually whisk in the oil. Season to taste with salt and pepper.

When the artichokes are cooked, remove them from the pan and leave them upside down to drain briefly. Then place them the right way up on warmed serving plates and, working round each one, push the leaves down towards the plate so they look like the petals of a flower, but don't break them off. As soon as you get to the smaller leaves, with next to no flesh at their bases and which are not worth eating, start to remove them until you reach the final cone of smaller leaves covering the choke. Pinch the pink tip of this cone between your fingers and pull it away in one piece. Scrape away the hairy choke from the base, pour some of the dressing into the natural dip of the base, and replace the cone of leaves as a lid. Serve straight away with the remaining dressing.

My main restaurant in Padstow, the Seafood, is pretty strictly for lovers of fruits de mer — we only have one meat dish on as a main course. But I always like to have on one or two non-fish first courses, too, because it gives the chefs a chance to work with meat, poultry and game, and this is one of those dishes. It is, I think, a pleasing combination of delicious crisp buttery Anna potatoes, dark red pigeon breast, seared and sliced, a little pile of leaves and a small amount of incredibly deep Cabernet Sauvignon made into a dressing with walnut oil.

Warm salad of wood pigeon with pommes Anna,
Cabernet Sauvignon, walnut oil and frisée *Serves 4*

4 x 45 g pigeon breasts
Olive oil, for searing
50 g prepared frisée (curly endive)
$1/2$ teaspoon extra virgin olive oil
Salt and freshly ground black pepper

FOR THE POMMES ANNA:
750 g small floury potatoes, such
   as Maris Pipers, each weighing
   90–100 g, peeled
50 g butter, plus extra for greasing

**FOR THE CABERNET SAUVIGNON
AND WALNUT OIL DRESSING:**
$1/2$ bottle Cabernet Sauvignon
2 teaspoons caster sugar
1 tablespoon walnut oil
2 tablespoons olive oil

For the pommes Anna, preheat the oven to 220°C/Gas Mark 7. Thinly slice the potatoes on a mandolin or by hand. Melt 25 g of the butter in a large, ovenproof frying pan, then remove it from the heat. Put 4 lightly buttered 9-cm plain pastry cutters into the frying pan, and neatly overlap a layer of the sliced potatoes in the bottom of each one. Season very lightly with salt and pepper and then continue to layer up the rest of the potatoes into the cutters, seasoning between each layer, until each one is about half full.

Melt the remaining butter and spoon it over the top of the potatoes. Transfer the frying pan to the oven and bake for 30 minutes until the potatoes are crisp and golden on both sides.

Meanwhile, for the dressing, put the red wine and sugar into a small pan and boil rapidly until reduced to approximately 3 tablespoons. Take the pan off the heat and very slowly whisk in the walnut and olive oil, and some salt and pepper to taste. Set aside.

Season the pigeon breasts on both sides with salt and pepper. Heat a thin layer of oil in a frying pan over a high heat, add the breasts and sear for 1 minute on each side, until nicely coloured but still pink and juicy on the inside. Remove from the pan, cover with foil and leave to rest for 3 minutes.

To serve, put the pommes Anna onto 4 warmed plates. Toss the frisée with a little oil and pile to one side of the potatoes. Carve the pigeon breasts on the diagonal into thin slices and tuck them in among the frisée. Whisk 4–5 teaspoons hot water into the dressing, to loosen it slightly, and spoon a little around the plate and over the pigeon. Serve straight away while still warm.

Light lunches

In a world of pizzas made with pineapple, hoisin-sauce-glazed chicken or sweetcorn and tuna, how could a simple bottom-baked dough tart made with just onions, garnished with a few anchovies and olives, be anything but rather dour? But not a bit of it. The combination of sweet onions and salty anchovies on crisp dough, hot from the baker's oven, is a truer reflection of the people and the lifestyle than any frothy combination of bright colours and flavours. For me, it sums up all that's best about street food.

Pissaladière
Niçoise onion tart *Serves 6–8*

275 g strong plain white flour
2 teaspoons easy-blend yeast
1 teaspoon salt
250 ml hand-hot water
2 teaspoons extra virgin olive oil

FOR THE TOPPING:
50 ml extra virgin olive oil
1.5 kg onions, halved and thinly sliced
A large bouquet garni of parsley,
  thyme, bay leaves, rosemary and
  oregano

2 teaspoons anchovy paste
6–8 anchovy fillets in oil, drained,
  and halved lengthways
Handful of small, black Niçoise olives
Salt and freshly ground black pepper

For the dough base, sift the flour, yeast and salt into a bowl and make a well in the centre. Add the warm water and olive oil and mix together into a soft dough. Tip out onto a lightly floured surface and knead for 5 minutes or until smooth and elastic. Return to the bowl, cover with clingfilm and leave in a warm place for approximately 1 hour, or until doubled in size.

Meanwhile, for the topping, heat the oil in a large pan over a low heat. Add the onions, bouquet garni and some seasoning, cover and cook gently for 45 minutes, stirring occasionally. Then uncover, increase the heat a little and continue to cook for 20 minutes or until all the moisture from the onions has evaporated and they are thick and pale brown. Remove and discard the bouquet garni, adjust the seasoning if necessary and set aside.

Turn out the dough onto a lightly floured work surface, knock out the air and knead briefly once more. Then roll it out into a rectangle and lift onto an oiled 30 x 37.5-cm baking sheet. Reshape with your fingers, then carefully spread with a thin layer of the anchovy paste. Spread the onion mixture evenly over the top, leaving a 2.5-cm border free all around the edge, then criss-cross the top with the halved anchovy fillets and dot with the black olives. Season lightly with salt and pepper and leave somewhere warm to rise slightly for 10–15 minutes.

Preheat the oven to 240°C, or as high as it will go. Bake for 15–20 minutes, until the crust has browned and the edges of the onions are starting to caramelize. Serve warm or at room temperature, cut into rectangles.

Previous page: Sunflowers near Toulouse

This recipe is a lot of fun, and based on the idea of a raclette. To me the problem with raclette is that the traditional Swiss cheese it's made with is not particularly exciting, and it can be rather indigestible too. Substitute a nice ripe washed rind cheese in a box, such as Camembert, or better still a Vacherin Mont d'Or, Swiss or French, and you have something all together nicer.

Baked whole Vacherin Mont d'Or
with new potatoes and gherkins *Serves 4*

1 x 250 g ripe but reasonably firm Vacherin or Camembert in its wooden box
1 teaspoon dry white wine

TO SERVE:
500 g small potatoes, peeled
125 g small gherkins or cornichons
Crusty French bread

Preheat the oven to 200°C/Gas Mark 6. Put the potatoes into a pan of cold, well-salted water, bring to the boil and cook for 12–15 minutes until tender. Drain, return to the pan, cover and keep warm.

Meanwhile, take the cheese out of the box and remove the paper wrapping. Take a thin slice off the top of the cheese, put it back on and return the cheese to the box. Pierce the top of the cheese a few times with a fine skewer and drizzle with the wine. Replace the lid and bake it in the oven for 15 minutes until the cheese is hot and has softened all the way through.

Put the cheese, in its box, into the centre of a large serving platter, uncover and pull back the top layer. Surround with the warm potatoes, gherkins and chunks of French bread for dipping and serve straight away.

Waterfront at Sète

Many people will say it's not possible to make proper Breton pancakes without the large, round, flat griddle they use, that you can't get the thin, lacy finish. But I haven't found that to be true, provided you keep your batter thin and use a little plain flour with the buckwheat. You will also need to flip the pancake over briefly because you won't be able to obtain the same intense heat as the Breton griddle. But I can think of fewer more satisfying regional pleasures than a couple of these galettes for lunch with a pitcher of ice-cold Breton cider.

Buckwheat galettes
with ham, egg and cheese *Makes 8*

FOR THE GALETTES:
75 g buckwheat flour
25 g plain flour
Large pinch salt
120 ml milk

120 ml water
2 medium eggs, beaten
25 g butter, melted, plus extra for
   cooking

FOR THE FILLING:
8 medium eggs
200 g thickly sliced cooked ham, cut
   into thin strips
200 g Gruyère cheese, coarsely grated

Sift the buckwheat flour, plain flour and salt into a mixing bowl and make a well in the centre. Mix the milk and water together and whisk enough into the flour to make a smooth batter. Then lightly whisk in the eggs and warm melted butter, but don't overbeat the mixture or it will become elastic and the resulting crepes will be tough. Leave to stand for at least 30 minutes.

Shortly before you are ready to cook the galettes, stir a little more milk and water into the batter, until the mixture has the consistency of double cream. How much you need depends on your flour and the size of your eggs.

Brush the base of a large (approximately 25–28 cm) non-stick frying pan with a little melted butter, pour in a thin layer of batter and swirl the pan so that the mixture lightly coats the base. Cook over a fairly high heat for about 2 minutes until lightly browned.

Flip the galette over and break one of the eggs into the centre. Break the yolk with the back of a spoon and spread over the surface of the galette to within about 2.5 cm of the edge. Sprinkle 25 g of the ham strips and 25 g of the grated Gruyère cheese into the centre and fold two opposite sides of the galette in towards the centre, still leaving the centre exposed. Fold in the other two sides (to make a square), flip over once more and cook briefly to heat the ham through and lightly melt the cheese.

Invert the galette onto a warmed plate and serve straight away. Repeat for the remaining galettes.

There's a perfect British substitute for a French ingredient in this recipe: Somerset 'Capricorn' cheese is as good as anything you are likely to find in France. It has exactly the right 'goaty' taste and a semi-hard texture that is just beginning to melt when the frying time is up.

Warm walnut-crusted goat's cheese
with beetroot and thyme salad *Serves 4*

100 g shelled walnut pieces

100 g fresh white breadcrumbs

4 x 100 g goat's cheeses such as
Crottin de Chavignol or Somerset
Capricorn, chilled

1 large beaten egg

100 g baby salad leaves

1 teaspoon extra virgin olive oil

Sunflower oil, for shallow frying

Salt and freshly ground black pepper

FOR THE SALAD:

600 g cooked, peeled beetroot

4¹/₂ tablespoons balsamic vinegar

3 tablespoons extra virgin olive oil

2 teaspoons thyme leaves

60 g very finely chopped shallot

¹/₂ medium-hot red chilli, seeded and
finely chopped

For the salad, thinly slice the beetroot and put the slices into a shallow dish with the balsamic vinegar, olive oil, thyme leaves, shallot, red chilli and some salt and pepper. Mix together gently and set aside until needed.

Preheat the oven to 200°C/Gas Mark 6. Spread the walnuts over a baking tray and roast in the oven for 10 minutes until lightly golden. Remove and leave to cool, then very finely chop and mix with the breadcrumbs.

Take a very thin slice off the top and bottom of each goat's cheese and then cut each one in half, horizontally. Dip the slices one at a time into the beaten egg and then the walnut and breadcrumb mixture, pressing it on well to give an even coating. Lay side by side on a baking tray lined with non-stick baking paper and chill for 30 minutes.

Shortly before serving, overlap some of the beetroot slices towards the outside edge of four 25-cm plates. Toss the salad leaves with the extra virgin olive oil and a pinch of salt and pepper and pile them into the centre.

Heat 1 cm oil in a large frying pan to 180°C. Add half of the goat's cheese slices, lower the heat slightly and fry for 2 minutes on each side until crisp and golden. Drain briefly on kitchen paper. Repeat with the rest of the cheeses. Push 2 slices of the walnut-crusted cheese slices in among the leaves and serve straight away, while the cheese is still warm and runny.

This is a light course that appears as a main course on our bistro menu. I often think that restaurant menus don't include enough dishes that, well, girls like. I'd be tempted to go for this type of dish more often myself, actually. No wonder Antony Worrall Thompson had such success in the early nineties with his restaurant the Menage à Trois in Beauchamp Place, which only did first courses. The essence of this dish is to get a good Toulouse sausage, which has a far higher proportion of lean pork meat to fat than usual sausages, often three times as much, and the fat is hard back fat and all is coarsely chopped by hand. Salt, white pepper, sugar and saltpetre make up the seasoning.

Hot Toulouse sausages
with a tomato, caper and shallot salad *Serves 4*

4 Toulouse sausages
Salt, sea salt flakes and freshly
  ground black pepper

FOR THE TOMATO, CAPER AND
SHALLOT SALAD:
4 vine-ripened beef or large tomatoes,
  thinly sliced
3 shallots, halved and thinly sliced
2 tablespoons nonpareilles capers,
  drained and rinsed
2 tablespoons roughly chopped flat-
  leaf parsley

FOR THE MUSTARD AND GARLIC
DRESSING:
1 tablespoon Dijon mustard
1 tablespoon white wine vinegar
1 fat garlic clove, crushed
6 tablespoons sunflower oil

For the dressing, whisk the mustard, vinegar and garlic together in a small bowl, then very gradually whisk in the oil to make a thick, emulsified dressing. Season to taste with salt and pepper and set to one side.

Grill or fry the sausages for 8 minutes, turning them over now and then, until nicely browned all over.

Meanwhile, overlap the tomato slices on a large, oval platter and sprinkle with a few sea salt flakes and ground black pepper. Scatter over the shallots and the capers.

Lift the sausages onto a board and slice each one on the diagonal into 4 pieces. Whisk 2 tablespoons of warm water into the dressing to loosen it a little, then drizzle over the salad. Arrange the sausages randomly over the top of the tomatoes, sprinkle with the chopped parsley and serve while the sausages are still hot.

I noticed during filming in France that steak tartare has become fashionable once more, so I hope it catches on again here in Britain. I suppose the idea of raw meat is a bit hard to take for some people, but it's always struck me as completely lovely. I think it's one of the best ways of using fillet steak, and when I was taught how to make it in the sixties, we always used the thin end of the fillet, the tail, the piece that you couldn't turn into tournedos. After that, it's a bit like making a bloody Mary with the judicious use of punchy ingredients, so I hope you like my version. Needless to say, it must be served ice-cold and always with a raw egg yolk nestling in an indent in the top.

Steak tartare *Serves 2*

300 g tail end of beef fillet, sirloin or
  rump, straight from the fridge
1 tablespoon capers, rinsed, drained and
  chopped
2 shallots, finely chopped
2 tablespoons chopped flat-leaf parsley
1 tablespoon extra virgin olive oil
1 gherkin or 3 cornichons, finely chopped

3 dashes of Tabasco
$^1/_2$ teaspoon sea salt flakes
20 turns of black pepper
2 medium egg yolks
Pommes frites (see page 200), *Melba
  toast* (see page 211), elongated slices
  of shallow-fried French bread or
  pumpernickel, to serve

Trim the meat of all fat and sinew and chop finely by hand or by using the pulse button on your food processor.

Put the meat into a bowl with the capers, shallots, parsley, oil, gherkin, Tabasco, salt and pepper. Mix together lightly with 2 forks, then spoon into the centre of 2 chilled plates and shape into a neatish round. Make a small indentation in the top and add an egg yolk to each one. Serve with one of the suggested accompaniments.

St Malo, Brittany

We've recently changed the menu at our second restaurant, St Petroc's Bistro, to be exclusively made up of French-influenced dishes, many of them coming from this book, and this recipe has been a runaway success. I think it makes a perfect light lunch, but we also serve it as a first course. The combination of black olive tapenade, with the bite of a big mushroom, parsley, the charred taste of grilled toast and some fruity olive oil is what modern, uncomplicated bistro food should be like. Incidentally, the perfect bread for this is Poilâne, as you want it to give you nice, long, oval slices. And if you like the idea of dishes like this, there's a brilliant little chain of restaurants called Tartine in London who do very satisfying combinations of hot and cold things on the same bread.

Baked field mushrooms with tapenade
on garlic croûtes *Serves 4*

8 large field mushrooms, each weighing about 100 g, wiped clean
3 tablespoons olive oil, plus a little extra for drizzling
4 x 1-cm-thick slices of rustic white bread, such as Poilâne

1 large garlic clove, peeled
Small bunch young flat-leaf parsley sprigs
Sea salt flakes, freshly ground black pepper and cayenne pepper

FOR THE TAPENADE:
75 g pitted black olives
4 anchovy fillets in olive oil, drained
25 g capers, drained and rinsed
3 garlic cloves, peeled
85 ml olive oil

For the tapenade, put the olives, anchovies, capers and garlic into a food processor and pulse 3 or 4 times until coarsely chopped. Then turn the processor on and add the oil in a thin steady stream through the lid to make a coarse paste. Stir in black pepper to taste.

Preheat the oven to 200°C/Gas Mark 6. Place the mushrooms on a lightly oiled baking tray, stalk-side up, and drizzle each one with about 1 teaspoon of oil. Dot each one with a teaspoon of the tapenade and season well with salt and the cayenne pepper and bake for 15 minutes.

Meanwhile, toast the slices of bread over a naked flame until nicely tinged with brown on both sides. Then rub one side of each slice with the whole garlic clove.

Put 1 slice of bread on each of 4 warmed plates and drizzle both bread and plate with a little more olive oil. Lift 2 of the mushrooms onto each slice of bread and pile a small handful of parsley sprigs on top of each. Serve straight away.

Wild ceps, Lot-et-Garonne

It goes without saying that this has to be one of the best omelettes in the world. I got the ceps from a roadside stall outside McDonald's on the road into Agen. I asked Bernard, the skipper of the Rosa, what the French thought of McDonald's, expecting a suitably outraged reply. 'They've got very clean toilets' was all he had to say. I've described as well as I can one method of making an omelette: folding the whole omelette mixture over into one third of the pan, then tilting the pan to form an oval shape up against the side before turning it over onto a plate.

Cep omelette *Serves 2*

100 g ceps
35 g unsalted butter
2 pinches of finely chopped garlic
2 teaspoons chopped parsley

6 medium eggs
Salt and freshly ground black pepper
Green lettuce salad with Orléanais dressing (see page 205), to serve

Brush the dirt off the ceps with a dry pastry brush and trim off the base of the stems. Then thinly slice them lengthways.

Melt 25 g of the butter in a large frying pan. Add the ceps, garlic and some salt and pepper and fry over a high heat until they take on some colour. Toss them over and continue to fry until golden on the other side and cooked through: about 3 minutes in all. Add the parsley, toss together briefly and set to one side.

For one omelette, beat 3 of the eggs in a bowl and season with a little salt and pepper. Heat a non-stick frying pan, which measures 18 cm across the base, over a high heat. Add 5 g of the remaining butter, swirling it around to coat the base and sides of the pan, and as soon as the butter is hot and foaming, put the pan back over the heat and add the eggs. Within about 6–8 seconds a thin layer of egg will have set on the base of the pan.

With the back of a fork, stir the eggs in a circular motion, at the same time moving the pan back and forwards with the other hand, to cook the eggs uniformly. While they are cooking, tilt the pan slightly away from you, so that the half-cooked egg starts to pile up. It should still be moist on top – *baveuse* is the word the French use for this.

Immediately spoon half the ceps down the centre of the omelette, then, using the fork, fold the side of the omelette closest to you over the mushrooms. Now run the fork under the far edge of the omelette and tap the handle of the pan to encourage it to move up the far side of the pan a little. Use the fork to fold the far side of the omelette back over the filling, making sure each end of the omelette comes to a point. Changing hands, hold the warm serving plate vertically against the side of the pan and turn the omelette onto the plate. Serve straight away with lettuce salad, and repeat for the second omelette.

This is a classic French bistro salad, and it's really all about the excellence of the leaves. It is depressing that in this country you can't buy the enormous variety of escarole, batavias, chicory, endives and dandelions you can buy in very small supermarkets and markets over there. Most of our supermarkets just give you bags of mixed leaves so hygienically washed in chlorinated water they taste of absolutely nothing.

Smoked ham salad
with shaved Gruyère, escarole and walnuts *Serves 4*

1 escarole lettuce or 2 English curly lettuces
100 g piece of Gruyère cheese
400 g (12 very thin slices) of good quality smoked cooked ham
10 walnuts in the shell (to yield 50 g)

1 small bunch chives, chopped

FOR THE DRESSING:
2 teaspoons Dijon mustard
2 teaspoons lemon juice
1 tablespoon red wine vinegar

2 tablespoons crème fraîche or soured cream
2 tablespoons extra virgin olive oil
1 tablespoon walnut oil
Salt and freshly ground black pepper

Remove and discard the outer leaves from the lettuce and break the remainder into leaves. Wash and dry well (in a salad spinner is ideal), if necessary.

Cut the cheese into very thin slices, using a cheese slicer, if you have one, or a mandolin.

For the dressing, whisk together the mustard, lemon juice and vinegar. Add the crème fraîche, whisk until well emulsified and then gradually whisk in the olive and walnut oil and some salt and pepper to taste.

Arrange the sliced ham, lettuce leaves and shaved cheese slices onto 4 plates and scatter over the walnuts. Drizzle over the dressing and sprinkle with the chopped chives.

I wrote this recipe for the fabulous and celebrated tomatoes around the Gascon town of Marmande, but any well-flavoured vine-ripened tomatoes would be almost as good. I see no problem in using a carton of fresh pesto from an Italian deli, or even pesto from a jar. Because it is cooked with the tomatoes, it becomes a flavouring element. So it's tomatoes, pesto, puff pastry and a little garlic and olive oil. That's it.

Marmande tomato tart
with basil and garlic *Serves 6–8*

500 g puff pastry
450 g large vine-ripened tomatoes, such as Marmande, skinned
2 teaspoons *Pistou* (see page 47) or pesto
1 small garlic clove, very finely chopped
2 teaspoons extra virgin olive oil
8 fresh basil leaves, torn into small pieces
Sea salt and freshly ground black pepper

Roll out the pastry on a lightly floured surface and cut out a 30-cm disc, using a plate as a template. Lift onto a greased baking sheet and prick the pastry here and there with a fork, leaving a 2.5-cm border free around the edge. Chill for at least 20 minutes.

Preheat the oven to 200°C/Gas Mark 6. Bake the pastry disc for 20 minutes, then remove and leave to sink down naturally. If necessary, press lightly here and there until level.

Thinly slice the tomatoes and discard the top and bottom slices. Dot the pastry here and there with the pistou and arrange the tomatoes, slightly overlapping, in circles on top. Sprinkle with the garlic, ¼ teaspoon of salt and some black pepper and drizzle with the olive oil. Bake for 5 minutes, then remove and sprinkle with the torn basil leaves. Bake for a further 5 minutes until the tomatoes are just cooked and the pastry is crisp and golden. Serve warm, cut into wedges.

Marmande tomatoes, Marmande, Lot-et-Garonne

This is a classic chicken salad you find in virtually every Vietnamese restaurant in France. What appeals to me about it is the combination of lightly poached chicken, beansprouts, spring onions and herbs with roasted chopped nuts and sesame seeds, together with the slightly gloopy fish sauce, lime juice and chilli dressing.

Vietnamese poached chicken salad
with mint and coriander *Serves 4*

50 g root ginger, peeled and thinly
  sliced
1 litre water
4 small, boneless chicken breasts
$^1/_2$ large cucumber
1 tablespoon sesame seeds
150 g fresh beansprouts
Bunch spring onions, trimmed,
  halved and finely shredded

Leaves from 1 x 20 g packet mint,
  torn into small pieces
Small bunch fresh coriander sprigs
60 g roasted salted peanuts, finely
  chopped

FOR THE DRESSING:
4 tablespoons Thai fish sauce
2 tablespoons red wine vinegar

2 tablespoons lime juice
2 tablespoons light soft brown sugar
$^1/_2$ teaspoon cornflour
1 medium-hot red chilli, seeded and
  finely chopped
1 garlic clove, finely chopped

Put the ginger and water into a large shallow pan and bring up to the boil. Add the chicken breasts and leave to simmer for 5 minutes. Then turn off the heat and leave them to go cold in the liquid.

For the dressing, put the Thai fish sauce, vinegar, lime juice and sugar into a small pan and bring to the boil slowly. Mix the cornflour with 1 teaspoon of cold water, stir in and simmer gently for 1 minute. Remove from the heat and leave to go cold, then stir in the red chilli and garlic.

For the salad, peel the cucumber, cut it in half lengthways and scoop out the seeds with a teaspoon. Cut the flesh into 5-cm-long matchsticks.

Heat a dry, heavy-based frying pan over a high heat. Add the sesame seeds and toss them around for a few seconds until lightly golden. Tip onto a plate and leave to cool.

Lift the chicken breasts out of the poaching liquid, remove the skin and pull each one apart into long chunky strips.

Loosely assemble the cucumber, sesame seeds, beansprouts, spring onions, mint leaves, coriander sprigs and pieces of chicken together on one large serving dish or 4 individual plates, and drizzle over the dressing. Scatter over the peanuts and serve straight away.

We don't have the same enthusiasm in Britain for Swiss chard and other members of the beet family that we have for beetroot itself. Maybe we think they are a bit bland, but if carefully nurtured and not masked by too many other flavours, they all have the same slightly sweet, earthy flavour. This tart, found all over France, is generally made with the white stalk only, but if you can get hold of young chard leaves from a farm shop – it's a vegetable that doesn't travel well and is therefore not usually stocked by supermarkets – use the green part too. This is a simple quiche but with the addition of a good quality Emmenthal cheese and a little nutmeg, and the loosely packed leaves give the tart a pleasing soft-set texture.

Swiss chard and Emmenthal tart *Serves 8–10*

1 quantity *Rich shortcrust pastry* (see page 211)
4 medium eggs, beaten
250 g Swiss chard, washed and trimmed

150 g coarsely grated Emmenthal cheese
300 ml double cream
10 rasps of freshly grated nutmeg
Salt and freshly ground black pepper

Roll out the pastry thinly on a lightly floured surface and use to line a greased loose-bottomed flan tin that is 4 cm deep and 25 cm across the base. Prick the base with a fork and chill for 20 minutes.

Preheat the oven to 200°C/Gas Mark 6. Line the pastry case with greaseproof paper, cover the base with a thin layer of baking beans and bake for 15 minutes. Remove the paper and beans and return the case to the oven for 3–4 minutes until lightly golden. Remove from the oven, brush the inside with a little of the beaten egg and return to the oven once more for 2 minutes. Remove from the oven and lower the temperature to 190°C/Gas Mark 5.

While the pastry case is cooking, bring a pan of well-salted water (1 teaspoon per 600 ml) to the boil and prepare the Swiss chard. Slice the green leaves away from the white stems, bunch everything up together and cut across into 2.5-cm strips. Add to the boiling water and cook for 3 minutes, then drain and refresh under cold water. Drain well, then press lightly to remove the excess water (give it a brief spin in a salad spinner if you have one).

Mix the chard with the grated cheese and spread loosely over the base of the pastry case. Mix the eggs with the cream, nutmeg, 1/2 teaspoon salt and some black pepper, and pour over the Swiss chard and cheese. Bake for 30–35 minutes until just set, covering loosely for the last 5 minutes or so if it is browning too quickly. Remove from the oven and leave to cool slightly before serving.

I still yearn for those dishes trendy in the eighties called feuilletés. Basically they were an update of the vol-au-vent, often in my case a vol-au-vent cut out to look like a fish. (I remember traipsing the streets of Paris looking for catering shops that sold such cutters. I found one in the end but it was too small.) Then feuilletés went out of fashion. Well, they were a bit rich, often filled with hollandaise as well as some delicate morsel of seafood or poultry. But I still love them, and this very pleasant combination of caramelized chicory and briefly sautéed chicken livers with a sauce made with reduced balsamic vinegar, chicken stock and parsley is just the right filling for the feather-light, crisp and buttery puff pastry. Let the chicken livers and sauce spill from the feuilleté on to the plate.

Sautéed chicken livers on puff pastry
with caramelized chicory and balsamic vinegar *Serves 4*

250 g butter puff pastry

450 g fresh chicken livers

4 small heads chicory

45 g unsalted butter, plus extra for greasing

2 tablespoons balsamic vinegar

80 ml *Chicken stock* (see page 208)

2 teaspoons chopped parsley, to garnish

Salt and freshly ground black pepper

Roll out the pastry and cut out four 9-cm discs. Put on a buttered baking sheet, prick here and there with a fork and chill for at least 20 minutes.

Preheat oven to 200°C/Gas Mark 6. Bake the pastry discs for 15 minutes until crisp and brown. Turn off the oven, open the door and leave them inside to keep warm.

Trim the chicken livers and then cut each one in half, slightly on the slant, into 2 thinner slices. Remove the outer leaves of the chicory if they are damaged and trim the bases if brown, but don't cut off too much. Slice each one lengthways into 3 or 4 slices so that each slice is held together at the base.

Heat 15 g of the butter in a large frying pan. Add the chicory slices and fry for 1 minute until beginning to brown. Turn over, reduce the heat to medium and season with some salt and pepper. Cover and cook for a further 3 minutes, then remove to a plate and keep warm.

Add a little more butter to the pan if necessary, then the chicken liver slices and fry for 1 minute on each side until browned but still pink in the middle. Season with salt and pepper and set aside with the chicory.

Return the frying pan to the heat, add the balsamic vinegar and let it bubble for about 2 seconds, rubbing the base of the pan with a wooden spoon as you do so to release all the caramelized juices. Add the chicken stock and continue to cook quite vigorously to reduce a little as you whisk in the rest of the butter.

To serve, slice each puff pastry disc in half horizontally and put 1 base each onto 4 warmed plates. Arrange the chicory and chicken livers on top, then spoon over some of the sauce and sprinkle with a little chopped parsley. Cover with the pastry tops and serve immediately, with some chilled Gewürztraminer.

Croûtes, grilled rustic bread rubbed with garlic and sprinkled with olive oil, are the French equivalent of the Italian bruschetta, and the sort of thing I have for lunch every other day. I've taken some of the flavours of a salad Niçoise – hard-boiled eggs, tomato, anchovy and onion – and made it into an appetizing open sandwich. This amount is perfect as a light lunch; for a more substantial meal it could serve two, with two sardines apiece.

Grilled sardine croûtes
with tomato, garlic, parsley and olive oil *Serves 4*

4 sardines, scaled and trimmed

Extra virgin olive oil for brushing and drizzling

Pinch crushed dried chillies

4 large slices of rustic white bread, such as Poilâne

1 garlic clove, peeled

1 romaine lettuce heart, broken into separate leaves

4 medium-sized vine-ripened tomatoes, skinned and sliced

1 *Roasted red pepper* (see page 210)

1 small red onion, very thinly sliced

2 hard-boiled eggs, peeled and sliced

4 anchovy fillets in olive oil, drained

Sea salt flakes and freshly ground black pepper

Preheat the grill to high. To butterfly the sardines, cut off the heads and then open up the gut cavity and put the fish belly-side down on a chopping board. Press down firmly along the backbone until the fish is completely flat, then turn the fish over and pull away the backbone, snipping it off at the tail end with scissors. Remove any small bones left in the fillet with tweezers.

Brush the sardines with olive oil and sprinkle lightly on both sides with the crushed dried chillies and some salt and pepper.

Toast the bread, under the grill, in the toaster or over a naked flame. Rub one side of each piece with the garlic clove, cut in half and put 1 piece onto each of 4 plates, putting the other 4 pieces aside. Drizzle lightly with olive oil and top each one with a few lettuce leaves, some tomato slices, a few strips of roasted red pepper and some slices of red onion. Drizzle with a little more oil and season lightly with salt and black pepper.

Put the sardines, skin-side up, onto an oiled baking sheet and grill for 3 minutes. Place on top of the lettuce, etc, on each plate, top with the eggs and anchovies and season with a little more salt. Rest the second pieces of bread alongside and serve straight away.

Fish and shellfish

This is not exactly the bouillabaissse they serve at L'Epuisette, the restaurant in Marseille where we filmed every step of the making of it. This is because most of us don't have access to small coastal rockfish like rascasse and weever, nor is it easy to get hold of the small crabs they also use in the stock. I've done my best, though, to achieve a flavour as close as possible to that excellent fish stew, which I ate with my friend, the chef Simon Hopkinson, at the end of my journey. I've also taken the deeply unPC step of using fillets of fish for the final cooking, simply because the business of finding small inshore fish will be so difficult for you – but if you are lucky enough to get them, use whole fish instead.

Bouillabaisse *Serves 8*

4 x 175–200 g small monkfish tails
4 x 250–300 g gurnard
4 x 250–300 g John Dory
2 x 500 g cooked lobsters
150 ml olive oil
1 medium onion, chopped
$^{1}/_{2}$ leek, cleaned and sliced
3 medium-sized carrots, peeled and
    finely chopped
$^{1}/_{2}$ small bulb fennel, finely chopped
Pinch crushed dried chillies

1 kg conger eel or pollack, skinned
    and cut into small chunks
100 g tomato purée
100 ml dry white wine
A bouquet garni made from thyme
    sprigs, bay leaves and parsley stalks
4–5 garlic cloves, coarsely chopped
$^{1}/_{2}$ teaspoon saffron strands
$^{1}/_{2}$ teaspoon mild curry powder
Salt, freshly ground black pepper
    and cayenne pepper

FOR THE CROÛTONS:
A little olive oil, for shallow frying
12 thin slices French bread
2–3 whole garlic cloves

TO SERVE:
100 g *Rouille* (see page 210)
25 g finely grated Parmesan cheese
450 g small potatoes (optional)

First prepare all the fish. Skin the monkfish tails and remove the fillets, and fillet the gurnard and John Dory. Break off the legs and claws of the lobsters and set aside the thinner legs for the stock. Crack the shells of the claws with the back of a knife and break at the joints into smaller pieces. Cut the rest of the lobster in half lengthways, detach the head from the tail and cut each tailpiece across into three evenly sized pieces. Put the fish fillets and lobster pieces onto a tray, cover with clingfilm and keep chilled until needed.

Now make a fish stock by putting the fish bones, lobster legs and 2.25 litres of water into a large pan. Bring to the boil and leave to simmer gently, uncovered, for 20 minutes, then strain into a clean pan. You should have about 2 litres. If not, make up with a little water. Set aside.

For the soup, heat the oil in a large pan. Add the vegetables and crushed dried chillies and cook gently for 20 minutes until soft but not coloured. Add the conger eel or pollack and fry briskly with the vegetables for 3–4 minutes. Add the tomato purée, white wine and fish stock. Bring to the boil, add the bouquet garni, garlic, saffron, curry powder and a pinch of cayenne pepper and leave to simmer very gently, uncovered, for 1 hour.

Meanwhile, make the rouille (see page 210) and the croûtons. For the croûtons, heat the oil in a frying pan, add the slices of bread and fry on both sides until golden brown. Drain briefly on kitchen paper then rub one side of each with garlic. Keep warm in a low oven.

Previous page: Fishing huts on the Médoc peninsula at the mouth of the Gironde river

Preheat the oven to 150°C/Gas Mark 3. Pass the soup through a sieve into a clean pan, pressing as much of the liquid through the sieve as you can with the back of a ladle. Return the soup to a wide-based, shallow, clean pan, season to taste with salt, pepper and cayenne pepper, and bring back to a simmer. Add the monkfish fillets and cook for 1 minute. Then add the gurnard and John Dory fillets and the pieces of lobster, making sure that they are fully submerged in the soup, and simmer for a further 2 minutes. The fish will still be slightly undercooked at this point.

Carefully lift the fish fillets and lobster pieces out of the soup onto a warmed serving plate, ladle over a small amount of the soup, cover with foil and put in the oven to keep warm, but don't leave any more than 10 minutes. Ladle the soup into warmed soup plates and serve as a first course with the croûtons, rouille and Parmesan cheese. Then serve the fish as a main course, with, if you wish, more rouille and some small potatoes cooked in the soup.

Right down deep in the Camargue there are a couple of shacks on the beach and a fairly rough-looking caravan site with lots of dogs and plenty of scruffy-looking kids. Beauduc is a smudge on the map somewhere between the Mediterranean and a network of étangs, the salt-water lagoons that are all part of Rhône delta. But there's a restaurant there called Chez Jou Jou, which is any seafood lover's dream: tellines (very small clams) with aïoli as a starter, then loup de mer (sea bass) as the main course – I don't know if there was any other choice, and I don't care really – all washed down with copious quantities of ice-cold Picpoul de Pinet. Jack Nicholson's been there, Dustin Hoffman's been there, and now me.

Chilled shellfish with creamy aïoli
and parsley sauce *Serves 6 as a starter*

1½ quantities *Aïoli* (see page 209), i.e. 300 ml
1.5 kg small clams, small mussels or cockles, or a mixture
150 ml dry white wine

500 g cooked shell-on North Atlantic prawns, heads removed but not the rest of the shell
3 tablespoons chopped flat-leaf parsley
Plenty of fresh French bread, to serve

First make the aïoli, according to the instructions on page 209.

Scrub all the shellfish with a stiff brush and pull out the beards protruding from between the shells of the mussels. Discard any that won't close when given a sharp tap on the work surface.

Put the shellfish into a large pan with the wine, cover and cook over a high heat, shaking the pan every now and then, for 2–3 minutes or until they have all just opened. Tip them into a colander set over a bowl to collect the cooking juices.

Return 3 tablespoons of the cooking liquid to the cooled pan with the aïoli and whisk briefly until smooth. Return the shellfish to the sauce with the prawns and 2 tablespoons of the parsley. Stir together well and leave to go cold but do not refrigerate. To serve, spoon the shellfish onto a large oval platter or individual plates and scatter with the remaining parsley. Serve with plenty of fresh French bread.

As someone who formerly eschewed cooked oysters is favour of oysters au naturel with lemon and nothing else, I feel a bit of hypocrite including a recipe for them very lightly cooked with a fluffy sabayon. But a New Zealand friend of mine was rhapsodizing nostalgically about Bluff oysters deep-fried in fish and chip batter so much so that I decided to include them in the repertoire of my fish and chip shop in Padstow. They are delicious – you bite through the crisp batter into the salty sea taste of an oyster. This dish is much more sophisticated but achieves the same feeling of excitement.

Warm Ile d'Oléron oysters
with champagne sabayon *Serves 2*

8 oysters

FOR THE CHAMPAGNE SABAYON:
200 ml champagne
Pinch caster sugar

3 egg yolks
75 g *Clarified butter* (see page 210),
  warmed
Salt and a little cayenne pepper

Preheat the grill to high. Open the oysters (see page 42) and pour away the juices from each one. Put them, still in their half shells, onto a large grilling tray, cover with clingfilm and set to one side.

Put the champagne and sugar into a small pan, bring to the boil and boil rapidly until reduced to 4 tablespoons. Pour into a large heatproof bowl and leave to cool. Add the egg yolks, place the bowl over a pan of barely simmering water and whisk vigorously until the mixture has increased enormously in volume, is thick, light and frothy, and leaves behind a trail when drizzled over the surface. Remove the bowl from the heat and very slowly whisk in the warm, clarified butter. Season to taste with a little salt.

Spoon 1 tablespoon of the champagne sabayon over each oyster and very lightly sprinkle each one with a small pinch of cayenne pepper. Place under the grill for about 30 seconds until lightly browned, and then divide the oysters between 2 plates and serve straight away.

*Le Pont Canal d'Agen,
at 580 metres the second longest
canal bridge in France*

I don't know if it's just me, but I found that some of the most satisfying meals I ate in France during the filming of the television series were those I had in the most unprepossessing restaurants. This lovely dish of clams was served at a roadside routier (a trucker's stop) at the end of the causeway that joins the Charente-Maritime to the Ile d'Oléron. The palourdes (carpetshell clams) were so fresh, just opened up in a bit of velouté with garlic and parsley. Could you ask for anything better to go with a chilled glass of Muscadet?

Clams in a garlic and parsley velouté

Serves 2

25 g butter
3 garlic cloves, finely chopped
1 large shallot, finely chopped
15 g plain flour

200 ml full cream milk
1 kg small clams, such as palourdes,
  washed
2 tablespoons dry white wine

1 tablespoon crème fraîche or
  double cream
1 tablespoon chopped curly leaf
  parsley

Melt the butter in a medium-sized pan. Add the garlic and shallots and cook gently for 4–5 minutes without letting them brown. Stir in the flour, leave to cook for a few seconds, then remove from the heat and gradually add the milk. Return to the heat and bring to the boil, stirring. Leave to simmer very gently over a low heat, while you cook the clams. The sauce should be quite thick now to allow for clam juices later on.

Put the clams and wine into a large pan, place over a high heat, cover and cook for 2–3 minutes, shaking the pan now and then, until all the clams have opened. Tip them into a colander set over a bowl to collect all the cooking liquid.

Stir 100 ml of the clam cooking liquor into the sauce with the cream and parsley and bring back to a simmer.

Return the clams to their pan, add the sauce and stir together briefly. Divide between 2 warmed, deep bowls and serve with lots of crusty bread.

I've done lots of experiments with white wines for fish sauces and I've come to the conclusion that Noilly Prat is the best. In fact, it makes very little difference to the finished sauce how good a white wine is (though this is not the case with red wine). However, the Provençal herbs and spices used to flavour Noilly Prat seem to add flavour to the reduction, and I've done my best here to create a simple homage to sauce vin blanc.

Fillets of John Dory with cucumber and Noilly Prat *Serves 4*

1 cucumber

25 g butter

4 x 450-g or 2 x 750–900-g John Dory, filleted

Salt, freshly ground black and white pepper

FOR THE SAUCE:

600 ml *Fish stock* (see page 208)

150 ml Noilly Prat

50 ml double cream

20 g chilled butter, cut into small pieces

1 tablespoon finely shredded basil

Put the fish stock and Noilly Prat into a saucepan and boil rapidly until reduced by three-quarters to about 180 ml. Now add the cream and continue to boil for 2 minutes. Remove from the heat and set aside.

Peel the cucumber and then cut in half lengthways. Scoop out the seeds with a melon baller or teaspoon and then cut each half across into slices 1-cm thick.

Preheat the grill to high. Melt the butter in a large heavy-based frying pan. Brush the John Dory fillets with a little of the butter, season on both sides with salt and a little ground black pepper. Place skin-side up on a lightly greased baking tray and set aside.

Heat the remaining butter until foaming, add the prepared cucumber and cook over a high heat for 1–2 minutes, shaking the pan every now and then, until lightly coloured. Season with salt and a little ground white pepper and remove from the heat.

Grill the fillets of John Dory: 2–3 minutes for those from the smaller fish, 5 minutes for those from the larger, until the skin is lightly browned and the fish is just cooked through.

Bring the sauce back to the boil and whisk in the butter, a few pieces at a time. Season to taste with a little salt.

To serve, place the John Dory fillets into the centre of 4 warm plates. Spoon the cucumber alongside the fish and sprinkle with the basil. Spoon the sauce over the cucumber and around the outside edge of the plates, and serve.

I made this with fresh ceps while I was in France, but sliced fresh chestnut mushrooms are a very good substitute. The inspiration for this dish came from an afternoon's fishing for trout in the upper reaches of the river Orb in the Montagne Noire of the Languedoc. I don't know why, but every time I'm filmed going fishing we never seem to catch anything. I was hungry at the time and full of anticipation and asked Sebastien, with whom I was fishing, how he best liked to eat fish. He replied, just with beurre noisette. I thought a simple stuffing of fried ceps and bacon would make trout even nicer, and indeed it does.

Fried trout stuffed with sliced ceps, garlic and diced bacon *Serves 4*

4 trout, each weighing about 300 g
40 g butter
60 g rindless streaky bacon, chopped
175 g fresh ceps, trimmed and cut
  into 4-mm-thick slices

2 garlic cloves, finely chopped
1 tablespoon roughly chopped parsley
25 g plain flour
2 tablespoons sunflower oil
Salt and freshly ground black pepper

FOR THE BEURRE NOISETTE:
75 g unsalted butter
2 teaspoons lemon juice
1 heaped tablespoon chopped parsley

First you need to remove the bones from the fish. To do this, remove the head of each one, and then, working with one fish at a time, start to cut the top fillet away from the bones until you can get the whole blade underneath the fillet. Then rest a hand on top of the fish and cut the rest of the fillet away from the bones until you are about 2.5 cm away from the tail. Turn the fish over and repeat on the other side. Then pull back the top fillet and snip out the backbone, close to the tail, with scissors. The fillets will still be attached at the tail. Repeat with the remaining fish.

Melt the butter in a large frying pan and as soon as it is foaming, add the bacon and fry briefly until lightly coloured. Add the sliced ceps and the garlic and toss over a medium-high heat for 1 minute until lightly cooked. Season with salt and pepper and remove from the heat.

Lay the prepared trout on a chopping board and pull back the top fillet of each one. Season the cut face of the fillets with salt and pepper and then cover the bottom fillet with a few slices of the ceps and bacon mixture. Sprinkle with a little parsley, cover with the top fillet and tie round the whole fish in two places with fine string to hold everything in place.

Season the outside of each fish with a little more salt and pepper, then dredge with the flour and pat off the excess. Heat the sunflower oil in one very large or 2 slightly smaller frying pans over a moderate heat. Add the fish and fry for 2½ minutes without moving them, until nicely golden. Carefully turn the fish over and cook for another 2½ minutes, until golden brown on the second side and cooked through. Lift the fish onto warmed plates.

Discard the frying oil (from one of the pans if using two) and wipe the pan clean. Add the butter for the beurre noisette and allow it to melt over a moderate heat. As soon as the butter starts to smell nutty and turns light brown, add the lemon juice, parsley and some seasoning. Pour some of the butter over each fish and serve.

This dish comes from a restaurant near Narbonne. Sea bass always tastes brilliant roasted with fennel herb, but the part of the dish that really enthused me was the little mould of Camargue rice cooked with some local olive oil. Somewhat irritatingly, the only Camargue rice you can buy in Britain is red – it is actually just brown rice with a slightly different-coloured husk. But for aficionados in the south of France, they also produce a small-grained rice that's very similar to risotto rice. This is not a really risotto, but a rice pilaf, whose ingredients are rice, water, salt and a lovely olive oil.

Roasted sea bass with pastis
and a Camargue rice risotto *Serves 4*

4 x 450-g sea bass, scaled
Olive oil for brushing
Large bunch fennel herb
4 tablespoons pastis, such as Pernod or
  Ricard
Salt and freshly ground black pepper
Lemon wedges, to garnish

FOR THE CAMARGUE RICE RISOTTO:
3 tablespoons olive oil
225 g Camargue rice, or risotto rice, such
  as Arborio or Carnaroli
475 ml boiling water
$1/2$ teaspoon salt

Preheat the oven to 220°C/Gas Mark 7 or as high as your oven will go. Brush each fish inside and out with olive oil and season inside and out with some salt and pepper. Push a small bunch of fennel herb inside the gut cavity of each fish and sprinkle it with a little of the pastis. Spread the remaining fennel herb over a large, oiled baking sheet and place the fish on top. Drizzle the fish with a little more oil and the rest of the pastis and set to one side.

For the Camargue rice 'risotto', heat the olive oil in a medium-sized pan, add the rice and fry gently for 1 minute. Add the boiling water and the salt, bring back to the boil, cover and cook over a low heat for 20 minutes. Then turn off the heat and leave undisturbed for a further 5 minutes.

After the rice has been cooking for 10 minutes, put the sea bass into the oven and roast them for 15 minutes.

To serve, lift the fish, together with some of the fennel herb, onto 4 warmed plates. Spoon some of the rice into a lightly oiled rounded mould, such as a non-stick mini pudding basin or ramekin, and press down gently. Turn it out alongside the fish, drizzle a little more extra virgin olive oil around the outside edge of the plate and garnish with lemon wedges.

This resulted from an idyllic eel-fishing trip in the Garonne. I must say the river fishermen of France seem to be a particularly peaceful and satisfied breed. A lovely afternoon, and plenty of eels for a change. I took them back to the barge and asked Bernard, the skipper, how he'd cook them. He obliged by serving them up for dinner like this. I think nothing could bring out the delicious quality of eel fat better than this simple sauté with garlic and parsley.

Sautéed eel with persillade *Serves 4*

450 g skinned eel on the bone
25 g plain flour, for dusting
10 g peeled garlic
15 g flat-leaf parsley leaves
1 tablespoon sunflower oil

50 g unsalted butter
Salt and freshly ground black
  pepper
Lemon wedges, to garnish
Crusty bread, to serve

Cut the eel across into 5-cm pieces, then dust them with the flour and knock off the excess.

For the persillade, put the garlic onto a board and crush briefly under the blade of a large knife. Add the parsley leaves and finely chop them together.

Heat the oil in a large frying pan, add the eel pieces and sauté on one side over a medium heat for 2–3 minutes, seasoning them lightly with a little salt and pepper as they cook. Turn them over, season once more and fry for a further 2–3 minutes until cooked through.

When the eel is almost cooked, take a second frying pan, add the butter and melt it over a medium heat. Add the persillade and cook very gently for 15 seconds to take away the raw taste of the garlic.

Tip the fried eel pieces into the second pan and toss everything together well. Transfer to a warmed serving plate, garnish with the lemon wedges and serve with plenty of crusty bread.

Ile d'Oléron

This recipe is based on one from the magazine Saveur, *which is in my opinion one of the best food magazines in the world. It always seems to find the real local food of any country and is not interested in faddy chefs. They took this recipe from a restaurant in Marlenheim in the Alsace called Le Cerf, which has memories for me of arriving on a very chilly November evening, with the smell of wood smoke and thoughts of sauerkraut, smoked sausages and those lovely fragrant wines including Pinot Noir that taste more like Gewürztraminer. If you ever needed examples of how terroir changes the flavours of wine, this would be it. I did this recipe with a fish caught in the Tarn at Moissac.*

Zander braised in Pinot Noir *Serves 4*

10 g dried porcini mushrooms
65 g unsalted butter
100 g thinly sliced leek
125 g thinly sliced carrots
75 g thinly sliced celery
75 g thinly sliced onion
³/₄ teaspoon tomato purée

¹/₂ bottle Alsace Pinot Noir or red
  Sancerre
300 ml *Chicken stock* (see page 208)
1 x 1.25-kg zander, sea trout or
  salmon, scaled and trimmed
2 bay leaves
1 large sprig of thyme

50 ml double cream
100 g chestnut or portobello
  mushrooms, wiped clean
  and sliced
2 tablespoons chopped flat-leaf
  parsley
Salt and freshly ground black pepper

Put the porcini mushrooms into a small bowl and cover with 4–5 tablespoons hot water. Leave to soak for 20–30 minutes.

Preheat the oven to 220°C/Gas Mark 7. Take a large roasting tin into which the fish will fit, add 50 g of the butter and melt it on the top of the stove over a medium heat. Add the leek, carrot, celery and onions and fry them gently until very lightly browned.

Drain the porcini mushrooms, reserving the soaking liquor, and thinly slice. Add to the vegetables and fry for 1–2 minutes. Add the tomato purée, Pinot Noir and chicken stock and stir together well.

Season the zander inside and out with salt and pepper, add it to the roasting tin and add the bay leaves and thyme. Bake in the oven for 25–30 minutes.

Remove the tin from the oven and carefully lift the fish onto a warmed serving dish. Cover with foil and keep warm. Strain the cooking juices from the tin into a pan, pressing out as much liquid as you can, add the porcini soaking liquor and the cream, and leave to boil over a medium heat until reduced to a well-flavoured sauce.

Meanwhile, melt the rest of the butter in a frying pan, add the sliced fresh mushrooms and some seasoning and fry briskly over a high heat for 2 minutes.

Stir the mushrooms into the sauce and adjust the seasoning if necessary. Spoon some of the sauce back over the fish and sprinkle with chopped parsley. Serve the rest separately.

I picked up the makings of this recipe from the chef on board the Anjodi, Louis, a Yorkshireman who has lived on the Mediterranean coast of France for seven years. He has an instinctive understanding of the local seafood cookery.

A little ragoût of seafood with fines herbes, white wine and linguine *Serves 4*

12–16 cooked langoustines or 100 g large freshly cooked peeled prawns
2 medium-sized squid, cleaned, to yield about 250 g
450 g small mussels, cleaned
2 tablespoons dry white wine
300 ml *Chicken stock* (see page 208)

150 g dried linguine
4 tablespoons olive oil
25 g plain flour
Small pinch crushed dried chillies
25 g butter
2 vine-ripened tomatoes, skinned, seeded and diced

1 garlic clove, finely chopped
20 g *fines herbes* leaves (parsley, tarragon, chervil and chives), finely chopped
1 teaspoon lemon juice
Salt and freshly ground black pepper

Peel the langoustines if using. Cut the squid pouches across into thin rings and separate the tentacles into pairs. Set aside. Bring a large pan of well-salted water (1 teaspoon per 600 ml) to the boil.

Heat a medium-sized pan over a high heat, add the mussels and the wine, cover and cook for 2–3 minutes, shaking the pan every now and then, until the mussels have just opened. Tip them into a colander set over a bowl to collect the cooking juices, and, when cool enough to handle, remove the meats from the shells, cover and set aside.

Pour all but the last tablespoon or two of the mussel cooking liquor (as it might be a bit gritty) into a small pan, add the chicken stock and bring to the boil. Boil rapidly until reduced to 180 ml, then turn off the heat and keep warm.

Drop the pasta into the pan of boiling water and cook for 8–9 minutes or until *al dente*. Drain well, return to the pan with 1 tablespoon of the olive oil, toss, cover and keep warm.

Season the prepared squid, toss with the flour and shake off the excess. Heat a large frying pan over a high heat, add 1 tablespoon of olive oil, half the squid and a few flakes of the dried chillies and fry over a high heat for 1 minute until just cooked through. Transfer to a plate and repeat with another tablespoon of oil, and the rest of the squid and chillies.

Now pour the mussel liquor and chicken stock reduction into the frying pan in which the squid was cooked and add the butter and the last tablespoon of olive oil. It will immediately boil. Add the tomato, garlic, fines herbes, langoustines or prawns and lemon juice and toss together very briefly until the prawns have heated through. Add the cooked mussels and squid, and toss together once more for about 1 minute. Season to taste with salt and pepper and remove from the heat so that the fish doesn't cook any further.

Divide the ragoût between 4 small, warmed soup plates and twist some of the pasta into a pile in the centre of each bowl. Serve straight away.

Landing the catch for bouillabaisse at Vieux Port, Marseille

During my travels while making this series I collected the postcards you find all over France that have recipes on them, accompanied by rather garish photos of the finished dish which would cause the modern food photographer a great deal of mirth. Why is it that the pictures in those old Breton or Provençal cookery books all look so brown? But the idea for this dish came from one of those postcards: a nice chunky bream, such as a dourade, baked with tomatoes. I've applied a bit of judicious cheffery by stewing the tomatoes with red peppers, garlic, thyme and olive oil first before roasting the dourade.

Roasted dourade
with sea salt à la Provençal *Serves 4*

4 garlic cloves, peeled

1 teaspoon fennel seeds, crushed

2 x 500–550-g dourade (gilt head bream), cleaned and scaled

Olive oil

Small bunch thyme sprigs

Fleur de sel or sea salt, and freshly ground black pepper

FOR THE PROVENÇAL SAUCE:

2 large beef tomatoes, such as Marmande, skinned

50 ml extra virgin olive oil

3 garlic cloves, finely chopped

1 large *Roasted red pepper* (see page 210), skinned, seeded and sliced into strips

1 tablespoon red wine vinegar

1 teaspoon thyme leaves

1 tablespoon nonpareilles capers

1 quantity *Saffron potatoes* (see page 201), to serve

Very thinly slice the garlic cloves and mix with the crushed fennel seeds. Brush the fish inside and out with olive oil and season with fleur de sel and black pepper. Now make 2 diagonal slashes across both sides of each fish, open them up and push some of the fennel-coated garlic into each one. Push 3 sprigs of thyme inside the gut cavity of each fish and place them on a large, lightly oiled baking tray.

Heat your oven to 220°C/Gas Mark 7 or as high as it will go. Slide the fish into the oven and roast for 15 minutes.

Meanwhile, for the Provençal sauce, cut the tomatoes in half and squeeze out as many of the seeds as you can. Cut the remainder into small chunks. Put the olive oil and garlic into a large frying pan and as soon as it starts to sizzle, add the tomatoes and roasted red pepper and turn up the heat. Toss over a high heat for 2 minutes, then add the red wine vinegar, thyme leaves and capers and toss together briefly.

To serve, pour the sauce down the centre of a large warmed serving platter. Remove the fish from the oven and lay them on top. Take to the table and serve with the saffron potatoes.

The idea that pasta was Italian food would be greeted with some surprise in Provence. It is impossible to say where pasta cooking stops or starts — but it's not on the border with Italy. I always recommend this way of cooking fish. Its great strength is that much as the dish is best made with fillets of really great fish, such as sea bass, bream, snapper or gurnard, it also works extremely well with bog standard fish fillets from the supermarket counter. I think it's the combination of the saltiness of the anchovies and the exoticness of the fennel that somehow makes the fillets of fish, all broken up in the pasta, taste sweet and delightful.

Provençal fish pasta
with fennel seeds, anchovies, tomatoes and olive oil *Serves 4*

500 g skinned fish fillets, such as cod, hake, sea bass or gurnard

4 vine-ripened tomatoes, weighing about 350 g

400 g dried long pasta such as linguine or spaghetti

5 tablespoons extra virgin olive oil

4 garlic cloves, thinly sliced

Good pinch fennel seeds (about $^1/_4$ teaspoon)

Good pinch crushed dried chillies (about $^1/_4$ teaspoon)

4 anchovy fillets in olive oil, drained and chopped

30 g flat-leaf parsley leaves, coarsely chopped

Salt and freshly ground black pepper

Green salad tossed with a little olive oil, red wine vinegar and salt, to serve

Cut the fish fillets across into 2.5 cm strips. Set aside. Halve the tomatoes and squeeze out most of the pips and juice. Roughly chop the remainder.

Bring a large pan of well-salted water (1 teaspoon per 600 ml) to the boil. Add the pasta and cook for 8–9 minutes or according to the packet instructions, until *al dente*.

Meanwhile, heat the olive oil in a large frying pan. Add the strips of fish and turn over rapidly in the hot oil, throwing in the garlic, fennel seeds and dried chilli as you do so. Cook for 3 minutes until the fish has turned white but is not completely cooked through. Add the tomatoes and anchovies and stir-fry for another minute. Season with salt and black pepper and add the parsley. Keep warm.

Drain the pasta well and tip into a large, warmed serving bowl. Pour the sauce on top and toss everything together briefly. Serve straight away.

Mediterranean fishing boats at Le Grau d'Agde

This is a dish local to Sète, which is often made with octopus. However, squid is much easier to get hold of here, and if anything it's nicer. This is a hearty seafood stew in the tradition of bouillabaisse (see page 86) and I'm particularly pleased with my addition of a small amount of star anise, which is in no way out of tradition with what the French themselves do in that part of the country.

Squid and potato stew with rouille

Serves 4

750 g unprepared large squid

5 tablespoons extra virgin olive oil

1 medium onion, halved and thinly
  sliced

3 garlic cloves, sliced

60 ml cognac

1 red pepper, seeded and thinly sliced

2 medium tomatoes, skinned and
  sliced

1 tablespoon tomato purée

1 pared strip of orange peel

1 sprig of thyme

1 bay leaf

2 'petals' of star anise

180 ml dry white wine

600 ml *Chicken stock* (see page 208)

250 g small evenly sized waxy
  potatoes, such as Charlotte, peeled

and quartered lengthways

5 tablespoons *Rouille* (see page 210)

Salt and freshly ground black pepper

2 tablespoons chopped flat-leaf
  parsley, to serve

Slices of pain rustique (rustic white
  bread), to serve

Clean the squid and cut the pouches across into 1-cm-thick rings and the tentacles and wings into similar-sized pieces.

Heat 3 tablespoons of the olive oil in a large deep frying pan. Add the onion and garlic and fry gently until soft but not browned. Add the cognac, light it with a match and shake the pan until the flames have died down. Then add the red pepper, tomatoes, tomato purée, orange zest, thyme, bay leaf, star anise, white wine and stock and bring up to a simmer.

Heat another tablespoon of olive oil in a frying pan, add half the squid and a little seasoning and stir-fry over a high heat for 2 minutes until lightly browned. Add to the sauce and repeat with a little more oil and the rest of the squid. Season to taste with salt and pepper, part-cover the pan and leave the stew to simmer gently for 1 hour, until the squid is tender and the liquid has reduced and thickened.

Meanwhile, put the potatoes into a pan of well-salted water (1 teaspoon per 600 ml), bring to the boil and simmer for 7–10 minutes until just tender. Drain well and set aside.

When the squid is tender, remove the orange zest and pieces of star anise from the stew, add the potatoes and simmer for 5–10 minutes so that they take on some of the flavours.

Meanwhile, make the rouille according to the instructions on page 210. Take the pan of stew off the heat and add 2 spoonfuls of the liquid from the stew to the rouille. Mix well and stir it back into the pan, but don't put the pan back over the heat or it might curdle. Adjust the seasoning if necessary, sprinkle with parsley and serve with plenty of bread.

I can't help feeling that sarladaise potatoes are the defining dish of south-west France. Interestingly, most recipes call for waxy potatoes, but I find that floury potatoes, such as King Edward's or Maris Pipers, produce a lovely sandy finish where waxy ones can be a bit too greasy. The combination of the tomato and capers, the sarladaise potatoes and the cod with a bit of bite to it is my idea of good bistro fish cooking.

Grilled cod on pommes sarladaise
with truffle oil *Serves 4*

4 x 175–225-g pieces of thick, unskinned cod fillet
15 g melted butter, for brushing
Salt and freshly ground black pepper

FOR THE POMMES SARLADAISE:
1 kg floury potatoes such as King Edward's or Maris Pipers

4 heaped tablespoons goose or duck fat
3 garlic cloves
25 g flat-leaf parsley leaves, chopped
1 teaspoon truffle oil

FOR THE TOMATO AND CAPER SALAD:
6 medium-sized vine-ripened tomatoes, thinly sliced

1 small red onion, halved and thinly sliced
2 teaspoons nonpareilles capers, drained and rinsed
1 teaspoon red wine vinegar
Pinch caster sugar
4 teaspoons extra virgin olive oil
1 tablespoon chopped flat-leaf parsley

For the pommes sarladaise, peel and thickly slice the potatoes – about 5 mm thick. Heat 3 tablespoons of the goose or duck fat in a large, reliably non-stick frying pan. Add the potatoes and some seasoning and fry over a medium heat for about 5 minutes until the bottom layer of potatoes is golden. Then turn the potatoes over and leave until another bottom layer is golden. Some of the potatoes will remain unbrowned, and as they cook the slices start to break up a little, but don't worry, this is how they should be. Repeat this for 15 minutes, making sure not to turn the potatoes before the bottom layer has browned. Then turn the heat down, cover and leave to cook very gently for another 10 minutes.

Chop the garlic and half the parsley leaves together to make a persillade. Uncover the potatoes and mix in the persillade and the truffle oil. Cover and leave to cook for another 10 minutes, or until the potatoes are tender when pierced with the tip of a sharp knife.

Meanwhile, brush the cod on both sides with the melted butter and season with some salt and pepper. Put skin-side up onto a baking tray and grill for 8–10 minutes until cooked through.

For the salad, arrange the sliced tomatoes over the base of a shallow serving dish and scatter over the sliced red onion and the capers. Whisk together the red wine vinegar, sugar and a pinch of salt and pepper and then gradually whisk in the olive oil. Drizzle this over the salad, scatter over the parsley and set to one side.

Now uncover the pan of potatoes, turn up the heat and add the last tablespoon of duck fat. Fry for 2–3 minutes until the bottom layer is crisp and brown, then add the remaining chopped parsley and turn over briefly. To serve, spoon the potatoes onto 4 warm plates and rest the cod on top. Serve with the tomato and caper salad.

I used to do a similar version of this dish in the early eighties but I've improved on it by adding two layers of spinach flavoured with some of the tarragon butter that also goes between the fillets. This is a high days and holidays dish. Might I suggest you consider it on Christmas Eve, accompanied by some steamed little potatoes and a green salad.

Salmon en croûte with tarragon butter
and wilted spinach *Serves 8*

2 x 550-g pieces of thick salmon fillet, skinned, cut from behind the gut cavity of a 3–4-kg fish; each should be about 20 cm long

500 g spinach, large stalks removed, washed and dried well

2 x 500-g packets puff pastry

1 egg, beaten

Salt and freshly ground black pepper

FOR THE TARRAGON BUTTER:

100 g unsalted butter, softened

1 tablespoon chopped tarragon

$1/2$ teaspoon salt

4 turns of the black pepper mill

1 tablespoon lemon juice

Trim the salmon fillets to the same size. Season each piece with $1/4$ teaspoon salt and some black pepper. Beat the ingredients for the tarragon butter together in a bowl.

Heat 1 tablespoon of the tarragon butter in a large pan. Add a large handful of the spinach and as soon as it starts to wilt, add more spinach, until it is all in the pan. Cook for 1 minute over a high heat, then tip into a colander and press out all the excess liquid. Transfer to a board and coarsely chop. Season to taste and leave to cool.

Cut a 350-g piece from one block of pastry (saving the rest for another dish) and roll out on a lightly floured surface into a rectangle about 4 cm bigger all round than the salmon fillets – a rectangle of about 20 x 30 cm. Roll out the second piece of pastry into a rectangle 5 cm larger than the first one – approximately 25 x 35 cm.

Lay the smaller rectangle of pastry on a well-greased baking sheet and spread half of the spinach mixture in the centre to form a rectangle the same size as the salmon. Put one of the salmon fillets on top, skinned-side down, and spread with the rest of the tarragon butter. Cover with the second fillet, skinned-side up this time, and cover with the rest of the spinach, trying to make sure that the spinach covers the salmon in an even layer.

Brush a wide band of beaten egg round the salmon and cover with the second piece of pastry, taking care not to stretch it or to trap in too much air. Tuck the pastry in well around the salmon, press the edges together to seal and trim away the excess to leave a 2.5-cm band all the way round. Mark the edge with a fork and chill in the fridge for 1 hour.

Preheat the oven to 200°C/Gas Mark 6. Brush the salmon parcel with beaten egg and chill for another 5 minutes, then remove and brush once more with egg – this will give it a nice deeply golden glaze. Then score the surface of the pastry into a tight diamond pattern with the tip of a small, sharp knife. Bake for 35–40 minutes.

Remove the salmon parcel from the oven and leave it to rest for 5 minutes. Then cut it across into 2.5-cm slices to serve.

It's ages since I've done an 'en papillote' recipe but they are so satisfying, especially if you take the puffed-up cases to the table and let everyone open their own to enjoy the aroma of fish, mushrooms, butter and wine. The parcels would be fine served on their own, but the beurre blanc is the perfect luxurious finish.

Hake en papillote with beurre blanc

Serves 4

2 small carrots, weighing about 75 g
  each, peeled
100 g celery sticks
150 g prepared leek
50 g butter
100 g button mushrooms, wiped and
  thinly sliced
4 pieces of thick hake fillet, each
  weighing 175–225 g

Olive oil, for brushing
Salt and freshly ground white pepper
Flat-leaf parsley sprigs, to garnish

FOR THE BEURRE BLANC:
50 g shallots, very finely chopped
2 tablespoons white wine vinegar
4 tablespoons dry white wine or
  vermouth, such as Noilly Prat

6 tablespoons water or *Fish Stock*
  (see page 208)
2 tablespoons double cream
175 g chilled unsalted butter, cut into
  small pieces

Pommes vapeur (see page 200), to
  serve

Cut the vegetables in half, and then lengthways into long, thin matchsticks. Melt the butter in a medium-sized pan, add the vegetables and cook over a medium heat for 5 minutes until just soft but not browned. Add the mushrooms and cook for a further 2 minutes, then season.

Season the pieces of hake on both sides with salt and pepper.

Preheat the oven to 240°C/Gas Mark 9. Cut out four 38-cm squares of greaseproof paper and foil. Put the foil squares on top of the paper ones and brush the centres with olive oil. Divide half of the buttery vegetables between the squares, spooning them slightly off-centre. Put the hake on top and spoon the remaining vegetables over the fish.

To form the parcels, bring the other side of the square over the fish so that all the edges meet. Starting at one end of the opening, fold over about 1 cm of the edge, doing about 4 cm at a time. Work all the way round the edge to make a semi-circular parcel. Then go around again to make an even tighter seal, and give the edge a good tap with a rolling pin. Put the parcels onto a baking sheet and bake for 15 minutes.

Meanwhile, for the beurre blanc, put the shallots, vinegar, wine or vermouth, water or stock into a small pan and simmer until reduced to about 4 tablespoons. Add the cream and boil until reduced a little more. Lower the heat and gradually whisk in the butter, a few pieces at a time, until the sauce is thick and creamy. Season to taste with salt and pepper.

Quickly transfer the puffed-up parcels to warmed plates and take them to the table. Instruct everyone to slit open their parcels, and to transfer the contents to their plates. Garnish with the parsley and serve with the beurre blanc and some pommes vapeur.

Over the years I have included many classic fish recipes from France in my
books. As this new book would be incomplete without these essential classics,
I have decided to repeat them here.

Dover sole à la meunière *Serves 2*

25 g plain flour
2 x 400–450-g Dover soles, trimmed and
  skinned
2 tablespoons sunflower oil
50 g salted butter

2 teaspoons lemon juice
1 tablespoon chopped parsley
Salt and freshly ground white pepper
1 lemon, cut into 6 wedges, to serve

Season the flour with $1/2$ teaspoon of salt and 10 turns of the pepper mill. Coat the Dover
soles on both sides with the flour and then knock off the excess.

Heat half the oil in a large well-seasoned or non-stick frying pan. Add one of the soles,
lower the heat slightly and add 10 g of the butter. Fry over a moderate heat for 4–5 minutes,
without moving it, until richly golden. Carefully turn the fish over and cook for another 4–5
minutes until golden brown and cooked through. Lift on to a serving plate and keep warm.
Repeat with the second fish.

Discard the frying oil and wipe the pan clean. Add the remaining butter and allow it to
melt over a moderate heat. When the butter starts to smell nutty and turn light brown, add
the lemon juice, parsley and some seasoning. Pour some of this beurre noisette over each
fish and serve straight away with the lemon wedges.

Moules marinière *Serves 4*

1.75 kg mussels, cleaned
50 g unsalted butter
1 medium onion, finely chopped

50 ml dry white wine
1 tablespoon coarsely chopped parsley
Crusty white bread, to serve

Put the mussels, butter, onion and white wine into a very large pan. Cover and cook over
a high heat for 3–4 minutes, shaking the pan every now and then, until the mussels have
opened.

Spoon the mussels into 1 large or 4 individual warmed bowls. Add the parsley to the
remaining juices, then pour all but the last tablespoon or two, which might contain some
grit, back over the mussels. Serve with plenty of crusty white bread.

Skate with black butter *Serves 4*

4 x 225-g skinned skate wings
15 g nonpareilles capers in brine,
 drained and rinsed

FOR THE COURT-BOUILLON:
300 ml dry white wine
1.2 litres water

85 ml white wine vinegar
2 bay leaves
12 black peppercorns
1 onion, roughly chopped
2 carrots, roughly chopped
2 celery sticks, roughly chopped
1 teaspoon salt

FOR THE BLACK BUTTER:
175 g butter
50 ml red wine vinegar
1 tablespoon chopped parsley

For the court-bouillon, put all the ingredients into a large pan, bring to the boil and simmer for 20 minutes. Set aside to cool, to allow the flavour to improve before using.

Put the skate wings into a large pan. Pour over the court-bouillon, bring to the boil and simmer very gently for 15 minutes, until they are cooked through.

Carefully lift the skate wings out of the pan, allow the excess liquid to drain off and then place them on to 4 warmed plates. Sprinkle with the capers and keep warm.

For the black butter, melt the butter in a frying pan. As soon as it starts to foam, turn quite brown and smell very nutty, add the vinegar, then the parsley. Let it boil down for a minute or so, until slightly reduced. Pour the butter over the skate and serve straight away.

Moules farcies *Serves 4*

48 large mussels, cleaned
1 large garlic clove
1 large shallot, halved

Handful of parsley leaves
Zest of $1/4$ lemon
100 g unsalted butter, softened

75 g fresh white breadcrumbs
Salt and freshly ground black pepper

Put the mussels into a large pan with 50 ml water, cover and place over a high heat for 3–4 minutes, shaking the pan now and then, until the mussels have just opened. Drain them in a colander, then break off and discard the empty half-shells, leaving the mussels in the other shell.

Preheat the grill to high. Very finely chop the garlic, shallot, parsley and lemon zest together (a mini food processor does this job well). Mix with the softened butter in a bowl and season to taste.

Dot each mussel with some of the garlic and parsley butter, then sprinkle with some of the breadcrumbs. Lay them on a baking tray and grill for 2–3 minutes, until crisp and golden brown. Serve immediately.

Grilled sea bass with beurre blanc *Serves 4*

1 sea bass, weighing about 1.5 kg
A little melted butter, for brushing

1 quantity *Beurre blanc* (see page 109),
   made with fish stock
Salt and freshly ground black pepper

Snip the fins off the bass, being careful to avoid spiking yourself, then scale the fish and remove the guts if necessary. Wash inside and out, and slash the flesh of the fish two or three times on each side.

Preheat the grill to high. Brush the fish with some melted butter and season inside and out with salt and black pepper. Put on a buttered baking tray and grill for about 10 minutes on each side, until the flesh is firm and opaque close to the bone and shows signs of coming away from the bone quite easily. Meanwhile, make the beurre blanc and pass through a sieve into a clean warm jug. Serve the fish whole and fillet it at the table onto 4 warmed plates. Hand round the beurre blanc separately.

Bourride of red mullet, brill and salt cod

Serves 4

25 ml olive oil
1 medium onion, chopped
1 small leek, chopped
$^1/_2$ bulb fennel, chopped
4 garlic cloves, chopped
2 pared strips of orange peel
2 tomatoes, sliced
1 fresh or dried bay leaf
1 sprig of thyme

1.2 litres *Fish stock* (see page 208)
$^1/_2$ teaspoon salt
225 g red mullet fillet, with the skin
   left on
225 g brill fillet, with the skin left on
225 g salt cod
225 g *Aïoli* (see page 209)
Chopped fresh parsley, to garnish
Boiled potatoes, to serve

FOR THE CROÛTONS:
25 ml olive oil
4 x 2.5-cm slices French bread, cut
   on a slant
1 medium-hot red chilli, seeded and
   finely chopped
4 sun-dried tomatoes in oil, finely
   chopped

To make the croûtons, heat the oil in a pan and fry the bread until crisp. Remove from the pan and set aside. Mix together the chilli and sun-dried tomato and bind with a little of the aïoli. Spread over the croûtons and keep warm.

To make the bourride, heat the oil in a pan large enough to hold all the vegetables, stock and fish. Add the onion, leek, fennel, garlic and orange peel and fry gently without colouring for about 5 minutes, then add the tomato, bay leaf, thyme, fish stock and salt. Bring to the boil and simmer for 30 minutes.

Add all the fish to the bourride, including the salt cod, and simmer very gently for 5 minutes. Remove the fish carefully and set aside in the warm serving dish. Strain the cooking liquor through a sieve into a clean pan, pressing down with a ladle to extract as much flavour as possible.

Put the aïoli in a large bowl and whisk in a good splash of warm stock, then pour in the rest, whisking continuously (if you add all the stock at once, the aïoli won't amalgamate properly). Return the sauce to the pan and, continuing to whisk, heat to the temperature of an egg custard (hot enough to be uncomfortable to your little finger) to thicken it. Pour the bourride over the fish, sprinkle with the chopped parsley and arrange the croûtons on top. Serve with boiled potatoes.

Sole véronique *Serves 4*

8 x 75-g skinned Dover sole fillets
A little butter, for greasing
600 ml *Fish stock* (see page 208)

75 ml dry vermouth, such as Noilly
** Prat**
300 ml double cream

25–30 seedless green grapes, halved
Lemon juice, salt and freshly ground
** white pepper**

Preheat the oven to 180°C/Gas Mark 4. Season the sole fillets lightly on both sides. Fold them in half, skinned-side innermost, and lay side by side in a buttered shallow ovenproof dish. Pour over the fish stock, cover with foil and bake for 20 minutes.

Remove the fish from the dish and put on a warmed serving plate. Cover once again with the foil and keep warm. Pour the cooking liquor into a saucepan, add the vermouth, bring to the boil and boil vigorously until reduced to about 6 tablespoons. Add the cream and a squeeze of lemon juice and simmer until it has thickened to a good sauce consistency.

Add the grapes to the sauce and warm through gently. Season the sauce to taste, pour over the fish and serve immediately.

La mouclade *Serves 4*

Good pinch saffron strands
1.75 kg mussels, cleaned
120 ml dry white wine
25 g butter
1 small onion, finely chopped

2 garlic cloves, finely chopped
$^1/_2$ teaspoon good-quality medium
  curry powder
2 tablespoons cognac
2 teaspoons plain flour

200 ml crème fraîche
3 tablespoons chopped parsley
Salt and freshly ground black pepper
French bread, to serve

Put the saffron into a small bowl and moisten it with 1 tablespoon of warm water.

Place the mussels and wine in a large pan, cover and cook over a high heat for 3–4 minutes, shaking the pan now and then, until the mussels have opened. Tip them into a colander set over a bowl to catch all the cooking liquor. Transfer the mussels to a large serving bowl and keep warm.

Melt the butter in a pan, add the onion, garlic and curry powder and cook gently without browning for 2–3 minutes. Add the cognac and cook until it has almost all evaporated, then stir in the flour and cook for 1 minute. Gradually stir in the saffron liquid and all except the last tablespoon or two of the mussel cooking liquor (which might contain some grit). Bring the sauce to a simmer and cook for 2–3 minutes. Add the crème fraîche and simmer for a further 3 minutes, until slightly reduced. Season to taste, stir in the parsley and pour the sauce over the mussels. Serve with plenty of French bread.

Oysters charentais *Serves 4*

20 Pacific oysters

FOR THE SAUSAGES:
350 g skinned belly pork, roughly
  chopped
75 g chorizo sausage, chopped

$^1/_2$ teaspoon each of salt, paprika,
  freshly ground black pepper, thyme
  leaves and cayenne pepper
100 g caul fat

Put all the sausage ingredients (except for the caul fat) into a food processor and process into a coarse paste. Scrape the mixture into a bowl. Cut the caul into 12 x 10-cm squares. Divide the sausage mixture into 12 pieces about the size of a golf ball, and shape them into small sausages. Wrap each one in a piece of the caul fat.

Twenty minutes before serving, carefully open the oysters (see page 42), taking care not to lose too much of the liquor. Divide them between 4 plates.

Preheat the grill to high. Grill the sausages, turning them now and then, until lightly browned and cooked through. Put 3 of the sausages on to each plate and serve immediately.

Marmite dieppoise *Serves 6–8*

100 g butter

2 leeks, cleaned and thinly sliced

2 bulbs fennel, thinly sliced

2 onions, thinly sliced

1 teaspoon fennel seeds, lightly crushed

2 teaspoons good-quality medium curry powder

175 ml medium-dry white wine, such

as Chenin Blanc or a Chardonnay from the Languedoc

2 tomatoes, skinned and roughly chopped

40 g plain flour

1.2 litres *Fish stock* (see page 208)

900 g mussels, cleaned

225 g monkfish fillet

450 g skinned cod fillet

225 g skinned lemon sole fillets

12 prepared scallops, each cut in half horizontally

450 g cooked langoustine

150 ml double cream

2 teaspoons lemon juice

$^1/_2$ teaspoon paprika

Salt and freshly ground black pepper

Melt 75 g of the butter in a large casserole, add the leeks, fennel, onions, fennel seeds and curry powder and cook gently for 10 minutes, until soft. Add 120 ml of the wine and the tomatoes and simmer until almost all the liquid has evaporated. Stir in the flour and cook for 1 minute. Gradually stir in the fish stock and then simmer gently for 15 minutes.

Meanwhile, put the mussels into a large pan with the rest of the white wine, cover and cook over a high heat for 3–4 minutes until they have opened (discard any that remain closed). Tip them into a colander set over a bowl to collect the cooking liquor. Keep the mussels warm.

Now strain the sauce through a conical sieve, pressing out as much liquid as you can, return it to the pan and add all the mussel cooking liquor except the last 2 tablespoons (as this might be a bit gritty), plus 1 teaspoon of salt. Bring back to a rapid boil and boil until reduced to 750 ml.

Meanwhile, preheat the grill to high. Melt the rest of the butter. Cut the monkfish into slices 1 cm thick and cut the cod and lemon sole fillets diagonally across into strips 2.5 cm wide. Put the monkfish and cod pieces on a greased baking tray and the sole and scallop pieces on a second one. Brush on both sides with melted butter and season well.

Cook the monkfish and cod under the grill for 4–5 minutes. Keep warm while you cook the lemon sole and scallop slices for about 2 minutes. Meanwhile, stir the langoustines, cream and lemon juice into the sauce and adjust the seasoning if necessary. Simmer for 1 minute, until heated through, then stir in the mussels and take the pan off the heat.

You can serve this dish up in one of two ways. For an elegant dinner-party type of serving, where you do all the work, arrange the pieces of grilled fish in the centre of 6 or 8 warmed plates and put a few of the langoustine and mussels in among them. Spoon over the sauce, sprinkle with the paprika and serve. Or you can simply add the pieces of grilled fish to the pot, carefully mix them in so that they don't break up too much, then sprinkle the stew with the paprika. Take the pot to the table and leave people to help themselves. Either way, you've still got all the beautiful flavours of the fish and shellfish cooked separately.

Here are a few other fish that go well in a marmite: Dover sole, hake, flounder, raw prawns, unpeeled North Atlantic prawns, clams and lobster.

Poultry and game

I have a feeling that people think that duck confit is a bit too cheffy. Well, it's not. In Lavardac market I picked up a recipe for salting duck legs for confit that only requires duck and sel gris, coarse unrefined rock salt from the south of France, and cooking the confit couldn't be easier either, as you will see below. It's best served, in my opinion, with a frisée salad and Constance Spry's recipe for braised red cabbage, which is sweet and sharp and counterbalances the fattiness of the duck. You'll notice that the cure requires a markedly small amount of salt, leading to a definitely cured but sweet confit.

Duck confit with braised red cabbage

Serves 4

FOR THE DUCK CONFIT:
4 large duck legs
100 g sel gris or rock salt
900 g duck or goose fat

FOR THE BRAISED RED CABBAGE:
500 g red cabbage, core removed
and the rest thinly sliced

1 medium onion, thinly sliced
250 g cooking apples, peeled, cored
and sliced
1$^1/_2$ tablespoons white wine vinegar
1$^1/_2$ tablespoons muscovado sugar
$^1/_4$ teaspoon mixed ground spices,
such as cloves, nutmeg and
cinnamon

$^1/_2$ teaspoon salt
Freshly ground black pepper
15 g butter

$^1/_2$ quantity *Frisée salad* (see page
205), to serve

Make the duck confit at least 24 hours before you want to serve this dish. Place one duck leg in the bottom of a deep plastic, glass or stainless-steel bowl, sprinkle with a little of the salt, turn it over, sprinkle with more salt and add another duck leg. Continue until you've used up the duck legs and the salt. Cover and leave in the fridge for 6 hours, turning the legs over halfway through. Don't leave any longer or the duck will become too salty.

Preheat the oven to 140°C/Gas Mark 1. Rub the salt off the duck legs and pat them dry with kitchen paper. Bring the duck or goose fat to a gentle simmer in a casserole dish in which the duck legs will fit snugly. Add the legs, making sure they are completely submerged, cover and transfer the dish to the oven. Cook for 1$^1/_2$ hours, then remove from the oven and leave to cool in the fat. Chill for at least 24 hours or until needed.

For the braised red cabbage, preheat the oven to 150°C/Gas Mark 2. Layer the cabbage, onion, apples, vinegar, sugar, spices, salt and pepper into a small casserole dish, dot with butter and cover with a well-fitting lid. Leave to cook for 3 hours, stirring once or twice.

To serve, you can reheat the duck in one of two ways. Preheat the oven to 220°C/Gas Mark 7. Lift the duck legs out of the fat and wipe off most but not quite all of it with kitchen paper. Put them skin-side up onto a rack resting over a roasting tin and roast for 15–20 minutes until the skin is crisp and golden and the meat has heated through. Alternatively, sauté the legs in a frying pan over a medium heat until crisp, golden and heated through. Either way they are delicious.

Spoon some of the red cabbage slightly to one side of 4 warmed plates and rest a piece of the duck confit on top. Pile some of the frisée salad alongside and serve.

Previous page: Lavender fields of Provence

119

I've already mentioned this lovely dish on page 16, but what really struck me about Vetou's cooking was that it was so uncomplicated. There are no elaborate stocks in this dish, but I do think that the simple, intense red wine sauce made à la minute, and in her case with a red wine from the Côtes du Marmandais finished with just a few 'pistols' of dark chocolate, was something quite special. I find it quite common with very good cooks that their natural talent makes everything seem effortless and wonderfully obvious.

Vetou's magret de canard
with red wine sauce *Serves 4*

8 dried Agen prunes

4 duck breasts, about 175–200 g each

150 g carrots, roughly chopped

1 onion, roughly chopped

3 shallots, roughly chopped

5 garlic cloves, roughly chopped

600 ml red wine, such as a
   Languedoc or Corbières

3 cloves

Large sprig thyme and 2 bay leaves

15 g plain chocolate

Salt and freshly ground black pepper

Pommes purée (see page 200) or
   Sautéed potatoes (see page 201), to
   serve

Put the prunes into a bowl and cover with cold water. Leave to soak for 1–2 hours.

Season the duck breasts on both sides with salt and pepper. Heat a large, heavy-based frying pan over a high heat. Add the duck breasts, skin-side down, lower the heat slightly and fry for 2 minutes until the skin is nicely browned. Turn over and brown them on the other side for 2 minutes, then lift onto a plate and set aside.

Add the carrots, onions, shallots and garlic to the duck fat left in the pan and fry over a medium heat for 10 minutes, stirring now and then, until soft and golden brown. Add the wine, bring to a rapid boil, then light with a match and shake the pan for a few seconds until the flames have died down. This burns off the alcohol. Then lower the heat, add the cloves, thyme and bay leaves, and leave the sauce to simmer gently for 10 minutes.

Return the duck breasts to the pan, skin-side down, cover and simmer for 2 minutes. Turn the duck breasts over, re-cover and cook for a further 2–3 minutes. This will give you duck that is still pink in the middle, but if you like it a little better cooked, cook for up to 1 minute more on either side.

Lift the duck out of the sauce onto a plate, cover with foil and leave to rest in a low oven (about 100°C) while you finish the sauce. Add the chocolate to the sauce and simmer for 2–3 minutes more. Then pass through a fine sieve into a small pan, pressing out as much liquid as you can with the back of a ladle. Drain the prunes, add them to the pan, and simmer over a medium heat until they have heated through and the sauce is nicely reduced and well flavoured. Season to taste with salt and pepper.

To serve, lift the duck breasts onto a board and carve, on the diagonal, into long thin slices. Lift each one onto a warmed plate and spoon 2 of the prunes alongside. Spoon some of the sauce over and around the duck and prunes and serve.

Henry IV of France was born in Gascony, and as I have come to really like the Gascon enthusiasm for good, honest cooking, so has Henry IV become a bit of a hero to me. First because in the fifteenth century, as king, he said during his coronation speech, 'I want every peasant to have a chicken in the pot on Sundays.' Secondly, in true Gascon style, he had such a love of garlic, particularly raw, that his bride Marguérite de Valois refused to share his bed on one occasion because of his bad breath. Would that this recipe from those times, a masterpiece of flavour, sensible nutrition and economy, could be as popular again in a world gone mad on fast food. Note that we've made my poule au pot with chicken stock rather than water. It produces a much better-flavoured soup. The idea, like a number of peasant and fisherman's dishes, such as bouillabaisse (see page 86), is that you serve the broth as the first course and the meat and vegetables as the main course sharpened with a sauce, in this case a mustard dressing flavoured with gherkins, hard-boiled eggs and parsley.

Henry IV poule au pot *Serves 6*

2.75 litres *Chicken stock* (see page 208)

3 x 1.5–2-cm-thick slices of *Home-salted belly pork* (see page 138) or rindless smoked streaky bacon

2 onions, quartered

3 celery sticks, cut into short lengths

2 turnips, peeled and quartered

8 carrots, peeled and cut into short lengths

4 small leeks, trimmed, cleaned and cut into short lengths

1 small head garlic, sliced in half horizontally

1 teaspoon black peppercorns

Large sprig of fresh bay leaves

1 x 2-kg organic free-range chicken, with its giblets

6 large or 12 smaller 2.5-cm-thick slices of French bread

Salt and freshly ground black pepper

FOR THE STUFFING:

The chicken liver, heart and gizzard, finely chopped

125 g fresh white breadcrumbs

60 g rindless thick-sliced smoked streaky bacon, chopped

60 g cooked ham, chopped

2 garlic cloves, finely chopped

30 g finely chopped shallots

20 g chopped parsley

2 medium eggs, beaten

1/2 teaspoon salt

THE VEGETABLES:

6 small carrots, trimmed and scrubbed clean

4 small turnips, trimmed and sliced

12 small evenly sized potatoes, peeled

12 small shallots or baby onions, peeled

4 small leeks, cleaned, trimmed and each cut on the diagonal into 3–4 pieces

1 head spring cabbage or equivalent weight of Savoy cabbage

FOR THE SAUCE GRIBICHE:

1 1/2 teaspoons Dijon mustard

1 1/2 teaspoons white wine vinegar

8 teaspoons extra virgin olive oil

1 teaspoon capers, chopped

1 teaspoon finely chopped gherkins

1 teaspoon finely chopped hard-boiled egg white

1 teaspoon finely chopped hard-boiled egg yolk

1 teaspoon chopped curly leaf parsley

Put the chicken stock, slices of salt pork or bacon, vegetables, garlic, peppercorns and bay leaves into a large pan or stock pot, bring to the boil and leave to simmer while you stuff the chicken.

Remove the giblets from the chicken. Add the chicken neck to the stock and finely chop up the rest of the giblets (liver, heart and gizzard). Put into a bowl and add the breadcrumbs, bacon, cooked ham, garlic, shallots, parsley, beaten eggs and $1/2$ teaspoon of salt. Season the cavity of the chicken lightly, spoon in the stuffing and then truss the chicken securely with string (see page 124).

Add the chicken to the pot, making sure that it is submerged, and add 1 teaspoon of salt. Bring back to the boil and leave to simmer for 30 minutes. Turn the chicken over, top up the stock with a little boiling water if necessary to keep the chicken covered, but don't dilute it too much, and cook for a further 10 minutes.

Meanwhile, preheat the oven to 150°C/Gas Mark 3. Place the slices of bread onto a baking tray and leave them for 30 minutes to dry out but not get at all brown. Remove and set aside.

Lift the chicken out of the pot briefly, remove the first lot of vegetables with a slotted spoon and discard. Return the chicken, bring back to the boil and add all the vegetables, except for the cabbage, and simmer for 5 minutes. Meanwhile, remove the outside from the cabbage, cut it into 6 wedges and remove the thickest part of the core but leave a little to help hold the leaves together. Add to the pan and simmer for a further 5 minutes, by which time all the vegetables and the chicken should be cooked.

Shortly before the chicken is ready, make the sauce gribiche. Whisk the mustard and vinegar together in a small bowl, then gradually whisk in the olive oil. Stir in the capers, gherkins, egg white, egg yolk, parsley and some salt and pepper to taste. Transfer to a small serving bowl.

To serve, lift the chicken onto a board, cover tightly with foil and leave to rest some-where warm. Put the dried bread slices into the bottom of warmed large soup plates or bistro-style bowls, ladle over some of the stock and eat as a first course.

Carve the chicken, then lift the salt pork out of the stock and cut each piece in half. Place some of the vegetables, chicken, salt pork and stuffing into bistro-style bowls and moisten everything with a few tablespoons of the broth. Take to the table with the sauce gribiche.

Garlic drying in roadside sheds

This really is a very good way of giving a simple roast chicken a spin of luxury. The mushroom and truffle paste I use is available in any good supermarket, and combined with the white truffle oil from Italy and some freshly chopped mushrooms, spread just under the skin of the breasts, imbues the white meat with a moist and earthy flavour. If you are lucky enough to get hold of pure truffle paste, use one teaspoon instead of one tablespoon. I've put a simple white risotto with the chicken, finished with some of the cooking juices. It is the perfect accompaniment, but if you don't feel like going to the trouble, use those precious juices from the roasting tin by making a simple gravy instead.

Roast chicken with chestnut mushrooms and truffle

Serves 4

40 g unsalted butter

35 g finely chopped shallots

2 garlic cloves, finely chopped

100 g chestnut mushrooms, finely chopped

2 teaspoons white truffle oil

1 tablespoon mushroom and truffle paste from a jar

1 tablespoon chopped flat-leaf parsley

1 x 1.5–1.75-kg organic free-range chicken

Salt and freshly ground black pepper

FOR THE RISOTTO:

1.2 litres *Chicken stock* (see page 208)

50 g unsalted butter

1 medium onion, finely chopped

300 g risotto rice, such as Arborio

150 ml dry white wine

25 g Parmesan cheese, finely grated

Green lettuce salad with Orléanais dressing (see page 205), to serve

Preheat the oven to 230°C/Gas Mark 8. Melt 25 g of the butter in a small pan, add the shallots and garlic and cook over a gentle heat until soft but not browned. Add the mushrooms and continue to cook for 7–8 minutes until the excess moisture has disappeared and you have a thick paste. Remove from the heat and leave to cool slightly, then stir in the truffle oil, mushroom and truffle paste, parsley, 1/4 teaspoon of salt and some black pepper.

Starting at the neck end of the chicken, slip your fingers beneath the skin and carefully loosen it over the breasts, taking care not to tear it. Push the mushroom and truffle mixture under the skin, spreading it as evenly as you can over each breast, and then truss the chicken into a neat shape.

To do this, place the bird on a board with its neck cavity and wings facing you. Slide a long piece of string under the chicken so that it lies around its 'waist', i.e. between the wings and the legs. Pull the ends of the string so that you have an equal amount on either side. Take one piece of string in each hand and run it along the gap between the legs and the body and under the end of each drumstick, towards the outside of the bird. Bring the ends of the string over the top of the drumstick ends and tie them together, as tightly as you can. Now pass each end of string down between the drumstick ends and under the parson's nose. Swap the string over to the opposite hands, bring together again over the top of the drumsticks and tie once more. Melt the rest of the butter and brush over the chicken and the base of a small roasting tin.

Put the chicken into the tin, season with salt and pepper and cover the tin tightly with a sheet of foil. Roast the chicken for 20 minutes, then lower the oven temperature to 180°C/Gas Mark 4 and roast for a further 50 minutes. Remove the foil cover and continue to roast the chicken for a final 15–20 minutes, until it is cooked through and the skin has nicely browned.

Twenty minutes before the chicken is ready, start to make the risotto. Put the stock into a pan and bring it up to a simmer. Keep hot. Melt the butter in a medium-sized pan, add the onion and cook gently until soft but not browned. Add the rice and turn it over for a couple of minutes until all the grains are coated in the butter. Add the wine and simmer, stirring, until it has almost disappeared. Then add a ladleful of the hot stock and stir over a medium heat until it has been absorbed before adding another. Continue like this for 20–25 minutes.

Meanwhile, remove the chicken from the oven and transfer it to a board. Cover it tightly with foil and leave it to rest somewhere warm for 10 minutes. Pour the excess fat away from the roasting tin, add a spoonful or two of the chicken stock and simmer over a medium heat, rubbing the base of the tin with a wooden spoon to release all the caramelized juices. Stir this into the risotto and continue as before, stirring constantly, until the rice is tender and creamy, but still a little *al dente*. Then stir in the Parmesan cheese and some salt and pepper to taste.

Carve the chicken and divide between warmed plates. Serve with the risotto and the salad.

I suppose you could say that this is a distant relative of coq au vin, but what I particularly like about it is the use of a sweet, unctuous Muscat wine, which, of course, ends in a slightly sweeter sauce. But this is balanced by plenty of lemon juice, which really brings the best out in a good chicken sauté, especially when it's served with some plainly steamed rice. I've chosen Muscat de Minervois as the wine because that's where I came across the dish, but you can make it with any sweet Muscat, such as Muscat Beaumes de Venise.

Chicken sauté with Muscat de Minervois
and crème fraîche *Serves 4*

1 x 1.5-kg organic free-range chicken
2 tablespoons olive oil
50 g butter
2 shallots, chopped
1 garlic clove, finely chopped
2 tablespoons Armagnac
¹/₂ bottle Muscat de Minervois

300 ml *Chicken stock* (see page 208)
1 sprig of thyme
2 bay leaves
150 g small button mushrooms, wiped clean
100 ml crème fraîche
2 egg yolks

1 tablespoon lemon juice
1 teaspoon *Beurre manié* (see page 210)
Salt and freshly ground black pepper
Steamed rice (see page 206) and *Green lettuce salad with Orléanais dressing* (see page 205), to serve

First, joint the chicken into 8 pieces. Lay the bird breast-side up and pull a leg away from the body. Cut through the skin at the joint, then pull the leg further away, cutting the skin to free it as you go. Turn the bird over and feel along the backbone for the soft oysters of meat. Cut under the oysters with the tip of the knife and remove them with the legs. Cut the legs into 2 pieces at the thigh joint. Remove the breasts still on the bone from the carcass in 1 piece by cutting backwards from the point of the breast down towards the neck through the ribs. (Save the rest of the carcass for stock.) Separate the breasts by cutting lengthways between them, and then cut each one in half on the diagonal so that each piece gets an equal amount of breast meat.

Season the chicken pieces well with salt and pepper. Heat half the oil and butter in a large deep frying pan and brown the chicken pieces on all sides. Lower the heat, add the chopped shallots and garlic to the pan and continue to cook for 2 minutes.

Add the Armagnac to the pan, set light to it with a match and shake the pan until the flames have died down. Add the Muscat wine, stock, thyme and bay leaves, bring to a simmer, cover and leave to cook for 30 minutes.

Meanwhile, fry the mushrooms in a little of the remaining butter and oil and season with some salt and pepper. Uncover the chicken, lift the pieces onto a warmed shallow serving dish and scatter over the mushrooms.

Mix the crème fraîche and egg yolks together in a small bowl. Remove the pan from the heat and skim any excess fat from the surface of the remaining juices. Stir in the lemon juice. Add the cream and egg liaison to the pan with the beurre manié, return the pan to a low heat and stir over a very gentle heat until the sauce thickens slightly, but do not let it boil. Season to taste with salt and pepper, then strain the sauce over the chicken and serve with the steamed rice and green salad.

127

This is the sort of dish I would always choose as a first course on a bistro menu. It was written by Debbie Major, who I work with on all my books. She was slightly nervous about what I would think of it, but I told her it was so good I rather wished I'd created it myself. Although we've suggested using a cast-iron griddle, it's actually a recipe made for a barbecue. The quails are best served a little pink.

Griddled spatchcock quail
with a red wine vinegar, shallot and mustard dressing *Serves 4*

8 quail
A little extra virgin olive oil, for
rubbing
Large pinch crushed dried chillies
Sea salt flakes and coarsely ground
black pepper

FOR THE RED WINE VINEGAR, SHALLOT
AND MUSTARD DRESSING:
2 tablespoons red wine vinegar
1 tablespoon Dijon mustard
6 tablespoons extra virgin olive oil
45 g peeled shallots, finely chopped
1 fat garlic clove, finely chopped
Large pinch cayenne pepper

2 teaspoons maple syrup
2 tablespoons chopped flat-leaf
parsley

Pommes frites (see page 200) and
some mixed salad leaves, dressed
with olive oil, to serve

To spatchcock the quail, turn them over so they are breast-side down, then cut along either side of the backbone with kitchen scissors and remove it. Open the bird out, turn it back over and press down firmly on the breastbone until it lies flat.

Rub the quail all over with a little oil and season quite generously on both sides with sea salt and coarse black pepper. Sprinkle with the crushed dried chillies.

For the dressing, whisk together the vinegar and mustard and then gradually whisk in the oil to make a thick, well-emulsified dressing. Stir in the shallots, garlic, cayenne pepper, maple syrup and parsley.

Heat a large ridged cast-iron griddle over a high heat until it is smoking hot. Put the quail skin-side down onto the griddle, lower the heat to medium and cook them for 5 minutes until they are nicely browned. Turn them over and cook for another 5 minutes. Then turn them over once more and cook them for 5 minutes or longer, until just cooked through – but don't overcook them.

Lift the quail onto a large warmed serving plate and spoon over the dressing. Cover loosely with foil and leave them to rest for 5 minutes. Serve with the chips and salad, together with lots of napkins and finger bowls, as this is finger food, not something to try tackling with a knife and fork.

Traditional barges on the Canal du Midi

One of my newly discovered French-market pleasures is the rabbit. This recipe comes from Kate Hill, an American food writer who has lived in Gascony for years and whose book, A Culinary Journey in Gascony, was very helpful to me – as was her house on the canal near Agen, where we filmed most of the recipes in the TV series. This is a local dish of rabbit, sautéed in duck fat and finished with a good regional red wine, prunes, carrots, onion, celery and herbs from the garden, then served with a local version of polenta called la cruchade. *Food doesn't have to be complicated.*

Rabbit with Agen prunes and polenta *Serves 4*

1 large young rabbit, jointed into 8 pieces (see page 132)

3 tablespoons duck or goose fat

50 g thick-cut rindless streaky bacon, cut into lardons (short fat strips)

6 button onions, peeled

6 shallots, peeled and split in two

2 tablespoons plain flour

4 carrots, cut on the diagonal into small chunks

2 fat celery sticks, cut on the diagonal into small chunks

Large bouquet garni made from thyme sprigs, bay leaves and rosemary

18 dried Agen prunes

Bottle of gutsy red wine, such as a Côtes de Gascogne

Salt and freshly ground black pepper

FOR THE POLENTA:

1.2 litres water

175 g polenta (not the instant type)

Unsalted butter, to taste

2 teaspoons salt

Season the rabbit pieces with salt and pepper. Heat a large, deep frying pan over a medium-high heat. Add the duck fat and bacon lardons and fry until golden brown. Add the onions and shallots and continue to fry until they are nicely golden all over, then lift everything onto a plate and set to one side.

Add the rabbit pieces to the pan and fry until lightly golden. Turn over and fry until golden on the other side, then sprinkle over the flour and turn once more.

Add the carrots and celery to the pan, together with the bacon lardons, onions, bouquet garni and half the prunes. Pour over all but 1 glass of the red wine (which is for the cook) to just cover the rabbit – if it doesn't, add a little water. Lay the rabbit liver on top if you have it, cover and leave to simmer gently for 1 hour, removing the liver when it's cooked, after about 10–15 minutes. You are not intended to serve the liver with the rest of the dish; it's more of a chef's perk, to go with the wine, while you are doing the cooking.

Meanwhile, bring the water for the polenta to the boil in a medium-sized pan. Very slowly pour in the polenta, stirring all the time, then lower the heat and leave it to simmer very gently, stirring now and then, for 1 hour.

When the rabbit is cooked, lift the pieces, together with the vegetables, out of the sauce onto a warmed serving platter, but leave the prunes behind. Cover and keep warm. Remove and discard the bouquet garni, and then crush the prunes into the sauce with the back of a wooden spoon. Add the remaining prunes to the pan, increase the heat and simmer quite vigorously until the prunes have heated through and the liquid has reduced to a well-flavoured sauce. Adjust the seasoning if necessary.

Stir a little butter, salt and some pepper into the polenta and transfer to a warmed serving dish. Spoon the sauce back over the rabbit and vegetables and serve with the polenta.

131

Pan-fried rabbit with tarragon sauce *Serves 4*

1 x 1.5-kg young rabbit
150 g carrots, coarsely chopped
2 medium onions (350 g), coarsely chopped
1 garlic clove, crushed
150 ml dry white wine

500 ml chicken stock
10 g sprig of tarragon
Bouquet garni made from 1 celery stick, 2 bay leaves and some parsley stalks
20 g *Clarified butter* (see page 210)

15 g chilled butter, cut into small pieces
Salt and freshly ground black pepper
Pommes purée (see page 200), to serve

Preheat the oven to 230°C/Gas Mark 8. To joint the rabbit, first remove the head, and then cut off the back legs from either side of the tail. Cut off the tail, and then the front legs. Trim away the bony ends of each leg, and the belly flap and ribcage from the body, then cut the remaining saddle across into 4 evenly sized pieces.

Put the trimmings from the rabbit (i.e. the end of the legs, the belly flap and ribcage) into a lightly oiled roasting tin and roast for 25 minutes. Sprinkle over the carrot, onion and garlic and roast for a further 15 minutes. Then remove the tin from the oven and place over a medium-high heat. Add the white wine and bring to the boil, rubbing the base of the tin with a wooden spoon to release all the caramelized juices. Simmer for a couple of minutes, then transfer everything to a saucepan and add the chicken stock. Strip the leaves from the sprigs of tarragon, coarsely chop and set aside. Add the stalks to the pan with the bouquet garni, bring to the boil, then reduce to a very gentle simmer and cook for 1¼ hours. Strain through a sieve into a clean pan, bring back to the boil and boil rapidly until reduced by about half. Set aside.

Season the pieces of rabbit with salt and pepper. Heat the clarified butter in a large frying pan, add the rabbit and fry for 5 minutes until the pieces are evenly browned all over. Cover, lower the heat and continue to fry gently for a further 20 minutes until cooked through.

Lift the rabbit onto a large warmed serving platter, cover and keep warm. Pour away any excess fat from the pan, add the rabbit stock and boil until reduced to a well-flavoured sauce. Whisk in the chilled butter, a few pieces at a time, together with the tarragon leaves and some salt and pepper to taste. Spoon the sauce back over the rabbit and serve with the puréed potatoes.

Many of my chef colleagues think that turnips are not a good accompaniment to anything simply because they can be overpowering, so it was with some misgivings that I first tried 'canard au navets', a speciality of Béziers in the Languedoc. As so often with French recipes, there's a subtle symbiosis between the two. I think it's the bitterness of the turnips which enhances the delicious fatty flavour of the duck, but I've added a few carrots too to counteract this bitterness with a bit of sweetness. This is a recipe for a duck designed to be served fairly well done, but cooking in a casserole in this way keeps it very moist.

Pot-roasted duck with turnips *Serves 4*

1 duck, weighing about 2 kg
1 tablespoon oil
200 ml dry white wine
400 ml *Chicken stock* (see page 208)
A bouquet garni made from thyme
   sprigs, bay leaves and parsley stalks

16 button onions, or 8 large shallots
   split in half
250 g small turnips, quartered
250 g carrots, cut into similar sized
   pieces
$1/2$ teaspoon sugar

50 ml Madeira
2 teaspoons *Beurre manié* (see page
   210)
1 tablespoon chopped parsley
Salt and freshly ground black pepper
Pommes purée (see page 200), to serve

Season the duck lightly, inside and out, with salt and pepper and then truss into a neat shape (see page 124). If your duck is not quite the weight stated above, calculate the cooking time allowing 15 minutes per 450 g plus 15 minutes and adjust the cooking times recommended below to suit.

Heat the oil in a flameproof casserole dish which is large enough to take the duck and prepared vegetables. Add the duck, breast-side down first, and brown well on all sides over a medium-high heat. Then turn breast-side up, lower the heat, cover and leave to cook for 30 minutes. Shortly before the time is up, preheat the oven to 200°C/Gas Mark 6.

Remove the duck from the casserole and drain away all of the fat into a small bowl. Set this aside for later. Return the duck to the casserole and add the wine, stock and bouquet garni. Season with $1/2$ teaspoon salt and 20 turns of the black pepper mill, cover and cook in the oven for 20 minutes.

Meanwhile, heat 3 tablespoons of the reserved duck fat in a frying pan, add the button onions or shallots and sauté over a medium heat until nicely browned on all sides. Remove and add the turnips, carrots and sugar and sauté until brown on all sides. Spoon the onions, turnips and carrots around the duck, and return to the oven uncovered for a further 25 minutes.

Lift the duck onto a warmed serving plate and surround with the onions, turnips and carrots. Skim the excess fat from the surface of the cooking juices, add the Madeira and bring to the boil on top of the stove. Simmer rapidly until slightly reduced and well flavoured, then whisk in the beurre manié and a little seasoning to taste.

Spoon a little of the sauce over the duck, sprinkle the chopped parsley over the vegetables and serve the rest of the sauce separately. Carve the duck at the table and serve with the vegetables and puréed potatoes.

Sunday afternoon card game on the banks of the Canal du Midi

There are really only two ways of cooking a partridge: roasting or pot-roasting. So there's a lot to be said for producing a nice gravy, or should I say, since we're talking French, a jus. Dubonnet, the ubiquitous red wine vermouth of France, is what I associated in the seventies with girls who didn't really drink. It always went with lemonade, but actually it's a drink with lots of flavour and it makes an excellent gravy with olives, smoked bacon, garlic and a little rosemary. Whether to choose grey- or red-legged partridges? The English grey-legged is smaller but has a sought-after, more gamey flavour. The red-legged is normally French and often farmed, and is bigger, plumper and slightly more tender. If you don't want to buy Dubonnet, ruby port is a good substitute.

Roast partridge with Dubonnet
and a frisée and watercress salad *Serves 4*

4 black olives, pitted and sliced

2 rashers thick-cut smoked streaky bacon, cut into strips

4 garlic cloves, sliced

2 shallots, sliced

The leaves from a 7.5 cm sprig of rosemary

4 partridges, preferably grey-legged, plus the giblets and livers from each bird (if available, but not essential)

A little softened butter for rubbing on the birds

50 ml Dubonnet or ruby port

300 ml *Chicken stock* (see page 208)

15 g chilled butter, cut into small pieces

Salt and freshly ground black pepper

FOR THE FRISÉE AND WATERCRESS SALAD:

100 g prepared salad frisée

100 g watercress sprigs

2 teaspoons extra virgin olive oil

1 quantity of *Sautéed potatoes* (see page 201), to serve

Preheat the oven to 230°C/Gas Mark 8. Mix together the black olives, bacon, garlic, shallots, rosemary and finely chopped giblets if you have them and spread the mixture over the base of a small roasting tin. Rub the outside of the birds with the butter and season with salt and pepper. Put them into the roasting tin and roast for 15 minutes. Then lower the oven temperature to 180°C/Gas Mark 4 and roast for a further 10 minutes.

Transfer the partridge from the roasting tin to a plate, cover tightly with some foil and leave somewhere warm to rest. Place the roasting tin over a medium-high heat, add the Dubonnet and rub the base of the tin with a wooden spoon to release all the caramelized juices. Add the chicken stock, bring to the boil, then transfer the mixture to a small saucepan and simmer vigorously until reduced and well flavoured. Pass through a sieve into another small, clean pan, pressing out as much of the liquid as you can with the back of the spoon, and simmer vigorously for a minute or two more until reduced to a well-flavoured sauce. Whisk in the chilled butter, a small piece at a time, and adjust the seasoning if necessary.

Put the prepared frisée and watercress into a bowl and toss with the olive oil and a small pinch of salt. Lift the partridge onto warmed plates and serve with the sauce, sautéed potatoes and the salad.

Meat and offal

It's not possible to get quite the right salted pork for petit salé in the UK. 'Petit salé' means lightly salted and our own streaky bacon, though the required cut, the belly, doesn't quite hit the spot. So, to make a perfect one, you need to salt your own pork. You also need some sort of chemical in the salt cure to keep the flesh pink. That used to be saltpetre, but you can't buy that any more because it was quite easy to make bombs with it. I tried explaining to the chemist that I'm a chef, not a terrorist, but it didn't seem to cut any ice. Fortunately there is a company (R. White Ingredients, Tel: 01706 226783) who produce a dry salt cure and it's well worth having a go. You will then be rewarded with a very satisfying dish.

Petit salé aux lentilles Salt pork with lentils *Serves 6*

1 x 1.5-kg piece of unskinned boneless belly pork
200 g dry salt cure (see above)
350 g Puy lentils
Bouquet garni made from thyme
   sprigs, bay leaves and parsley stalks
12 small shallots or button onions,
   peeled

6 small carrots, cut on the diagonal
   into 5-cm pieces
3–4 fat celery sticks, cut on the
   diagonal into 5-cm pieces
1 x 225-g piece of smoked pork
   sausage
Good handful of coarsely chopped
   parsley

25 g unsalted butter
Freshly ground black pepper
Steamed green cabbage (see page
   204), to serve

To salt the pork, put the piece of belly into a shallow dish and sprinkle over half of the dry salt cure. Rub it well into the meat, then turn over and repeat with the remainder. Cover with clingfilm and set aside in the fridge for 4 hours.

Lift the pork out of the now slightly dissolved cure and rinse off the excess. Put it into a medium-sized flameproof casserole dish, cover with 1.75 litres of fresh water and bring to the boil, skimming off any scum as it rises to the surface. Cover and leave to simmer gently for 45 minutes to 1 hour.

Add the lentils and bouquet garni to the casserole and simmer, uncovered, for 15 minutes until they are about half cooked. Then add the shallots or button onions, carrots, celery and smoked pork sausage and simmer for a further 20 minutes until the vegetables and lentils are cooked and the liquid has reduced.

Remove the piece of pork and the sausage from the lentils. Cut the pork across into thick slices and the sausage on the diagonal into pieces. Stir the parsley, butter and some freshly ground black pepper into the lentils and, using a slotted spoon, spoon some into the centre of 6 warmed bistro-style plates. Rest some of the sliced pork and sausage on top. Serve with some simply steamed cabbage and Dijon mustard.

Tip: You can make this dish with a piece of unsmoked streaky bacon. Carve off a thin slice, drop it into a pan of simmering water and simmer for a minute or two, then taste. If it is very salty, cover the bacon with plenty of cold water and leave to soak for 1 hour, changing the water halfway through. Then continue as for the recipe above.

Previous page: Panoramic view towards the hill town of Monflanquin from the hillside named Bellevue in Lot-et-Garonne

A recipe for cassoulet is a bit like a recipe for bouillabaisse: difficult because everyone has their own version and much intolerance abounds. Mine is based on many examples I tried around the town of Castelnaudary where they tend to keep things fairly straightforward and where they frown on the use of a breadcrumb crust. The essence of it seems to me to be the symbiosis of pork, duck fat, beans and garlic, and as with other famous dishes I see my job mainly as removing unwanted ingredients to get back to the essence of what the original dish was about. Do you know, the first time I tried cassoulet I was struck by how much it's the same sort of dish as Lancashire hot-pot? I'm an extreme fan of both.

Cassoulet *Serves 8*

500 g *Home-salted belly pork* (see page 138)
65 g duck or goose fat
1 head garlic, broken into cloves, peeled and sliced
1 large onion, chopped

1 kg dried haricots blancs beans, soaked overnight
Large bouquet garni made from leek, celery, thyme sprigs, bay leaves and parsley stalks
6 good-quality Toulouse sausages

4 legs of *Duck confit* (see page 119), cut into 2 at the joint

Cut the piece of belly pork lengthways into 3 thick slices, then cut each piece across into two. Preheat the oven to 180°C/Gas Mark 4. Heat 50 g of the duck fat in a 6-litre flame-proof casserole dish. Add the garlic and onion and fry gently until soft but not browned. Add the beans and the pieces of salted belly pork, cover with 1.75 litres water and push in the bouquet garni. Bring to the boil, skimming off any scum as it rises to the surface, then cover, transfer to the oven and bake for 1 hour or until the beans are just tender – this will depend on the age of your beans.

Heat the remaining duck fat in a frying pan and brown the sausages all over. Lift them onto a board and slice each one sharply on the diagonal into 3 pieces.

Remove the cassoulet from the oven and increase the oven temperature to 220°C/Gas Mark 7. Add the sausages and the pieces of duck confit to the casserole and push them down well into the beans. Return the casserole to the oven and bake uncovered for a further 45 minutes or until the liquid has reduced and the cassoulet is covered in a dark golden crust. Serve straight from the pot at the table.

Homemade cassoulet, bottled and sold in the market

Ragoût of lamb with Provençal rosé wine, tomatoes and flageolets *Serves 4*

225 g dried flageolet beans, soaked
  overnight in plenty of cold water
1 large shoulder of lamb, weighing
  about 2 kg
3 tablespoons olive oil
2 medium onions, chopped
5 garlic cloves, finely chopped
1 tablespoon tomato purée
500 g vine-ripened tomatoes,

skinned, seeded and roughly
  chopped
2 tablespoons plain flour
300 ml rosé wine
600 ml *Chicken stock* (see page 208)
Bouquet garni made from thyme
  sprigs and bay leaves
Sea salt and freshly ground black
  pepper

FOR THE PERSILLADE:
2 garlic cloves
Large handful of flat-leaf parsley
  leaves

400 g cooked tubetti pasta tossed
  with a little butter, to serve

Drain the beans, put them into a pan and cover with plenty of fresh water. Bring to the boil, skimming off any scum as it rises to the surface, and leave to simmer until the beans are tender. This could take anywhere between 45 minutes and 1$^{1}/_{2}$ hours, depending on the age of your beans. Drain, cover and set aside.

Bone out the shoulder of lamb and trim away all the excess fat and the skin from the meat. Cut it into 5–6-cm chunks and season with salt and pepper.

Heat 2 tablespoons of the olive oil in a large flameproof casserole. Add half the lamb and fry over a medium-high heat until nicely browned on all sides. Lift onto a plate and repeat with the rest of the lamb.

Add the remaining olive oil, onions and garlic to the casserole and fry until lightly golden. Add the tomato purée and tomatoes and fry for 2 minutes. Stir in the flour and cook for 1–2 minutes, then return the lamb to the pan, pour over the wine and bring to the boil. Simmer rapidly until the wine has reduced by half.

Pour over enough stock to barely cover the meat and add the bouquet garni, 1 teaspoon sea salt and 20 turns of black pepper. Part cover and simmer gently for 1 hour or until the lamb is tender and the sauce has reduced and thickened.

Add the cooked flageolet beans and simmer uncovered for a further 5–10 minutes until the beans have heated through. Adjust the seasoning if necessary.

For the persillade, crush the garlic cloves on a board under the blade of a large knife, add the parsley leaves and chop together finely. Sprinkle this over the ragoût and serve at the table with the cooked tubetti pasta.

La Cité de Carcassonne, the old medieval walled town viewed across a field of sunflowers

This recipe is the result of a collaboration between David Pritchard (the director) and me. When he told me about the dish, which he had cooked back at home in Plymouth, I was initially a little sceptical. I'm not a fan of stewed pork, but he insisted, asserting that what makes this dish so special is the garlic, and I have to admit he's right. The garlic becomes sweet and subtle in the stewing. It's amazingly easy to make and I do think it's the sort of dish those bargees, with their horses plodding down the towpath, would have cooked up in their galleys. David used butter beans for this, the ones you can buy in fancy glass jars, but I've adapted it to use haricots. But use butter beans if you prefer.

Bargee's pork and garlic stew *Serves 4–6*

500 g dried haricot blanc beans,
  soaked overnight
1 x 1.6-kg loin of pork on the bone
3 tablespoons olive oil
2 heads garlic, cloves peeled and
  thinly sliced
120 ml dry white wine
450 g vine-ripened tomatoes,

skinned and chopped
4–5 tablespoons chopped parsley
25 g butter
Salt and freshly ground black pepper

FOR THE STOCK:
The bones from the pork loin (see
  method, below)

750 g chicken wings
1 large onion, sliced
3 sticks celery, sliced
250 g carrots, sliced
3 tomatoes, sliced
2 bay leaves
6–8 black peppercorns
A large handful of parsley stalks

Gilles Pons harvesting the grapes in his vineyard Gaillot, in Casseneuil, Lot-et-Garonne

First make the stock. Cut the meat away from the bones of the pork loin in one large piece, then remove and discard the skin and all the excess fat from the meat and cut it into 4-cm chunks. Cover and chill until needed. Put the pork bones, chicken wings, onion, celery, carrots, tomatoes, bay leaves, peppercorns and parsley stalks into a large pan and cover with 2.5 litres water. Bring to a simmer, skimming off the scum as it rises to the surface, and leave to simmer for 2 hours. Then strain into a clean pan and boil rapidly until reduced to 600 ml.

Meanwhile, drain the soaked beans, tip them into a large pan and cover with plenty of fresh water. Bring to the boil, again skimming off the scum as it comes to the surface, and leave them to simmer for about 1 hour or until tender. This will depend on the age of your beans. Then drain and set to one side.

Heat the olive oil in a large flameproof casserole. Add half the pork pieces and some seasoning and brown them well on all sides. Lift onto a plate and repeat with the rest of the pork. Return all the pork to the pan with half of the sliced garlic, lower the heat slightly and fry for 5 minutes, taking care not to let the garlic get too brown or it will start to taste bitter. Add the white wine, increase the heat again slightly, and cook rapidly until it has almost disappeared. Then add the tomatoes, and cook for a further 5 minutes, until they have broken down into a sauce. Now add the cooked beans, reduced stock, remaining sliced garlic and some seasoning, bring back to a simmer and leave the stew to cook for 30 minutes until the sauce has reduced and thickened to a good consistency and the pork is tender. Stir in the chopped parsley and butter and adjust the seasoning if necessary.

This dish is known as daube de taureau *in the Camargue. I had the mistaken belief that it was traditionally made with the beef left over from the bull fights, and I'm sure I picked up an idea that it was supposed to endow consumers with machismo. Actually it is traditionally made with beef from a breed of bull bred for bullfighting, but really what counts in this dish are the flavourings of a deep red wine such as Corbières, cinnamon, cloves and Provençal herbs. I must say when I had this dish in Le Sambuc near Arles, having just witnessed the round-up of the same bulls on a hot afternoon by very tough-looking locals on white Camargue horses, it did seem like the most authentically Provençal beef stew I'd ever tasted. I've served this with macaronade, a delicious local side dish of macaroni moistened with some of the rich gravy from the stew, layered with Parmesan and then grilled.*

Bullfighter's beef stew with macaronade

Serves 8

1.5 kg chuck or blade steak, cut into 5-cm chunks
2 medium onions, chopped
6 garlic cloves, crushed
2 peeled carrots, cut on the diagonal into slices
1 bottle red wine such as Corbières
2 large sprigs of thyme
1 large sprig of rosemary

2 bay leaves
¹/₂ teaspoon dried thyme
6 cloves
7.5-cm piece cinnamon stick
3 tablespoons olive oil
75 g knuckle end of Parma ham or pancetta, diced
50 g small black olives in olive oil, drained

1 tablespoon *Beurre manié* (see page 210)
Salt and freshly ground black pepper

FOR THE MACARONADE:
500 g macaroni
250 ml of the liquid from the stew
75 g Parmesan cheese, finely grated

Put the beef into a large bowl with the onions, garlic, carrots, red wine, a bouquet garni of the thyme, rosemary and bay leaves, the dried thyme, cloves and cinnamon stick. Cover and leave to marinate in the fridge for 24 hours, stirring once or twice.

The next day, tip the meat and vegetables into a colander set over a bowl and leave to drain well. Heat 2 tablespoons of the olive oil in a large flameproof casserole, add half of the beef pieces and fry until nicely browned all over, seasoning as you do so. Lift onto a plate and repeat with the rest of the beef.

Add the remaining oil and the diced Parma ham or pancetta to the casserole and fry briefly until golden. Add the drained vegetables from the marinade and fry briefly until the onions have taken on a little colour and are beginning to soften.

Return the beef to the casserole with the reserved marinade, black olives, 1 teaspoon of salt and 20 turns of the black pepper mill. Bring to the boil, then lower the heat, cover and leave to simmer gently for 2–2¹/₂ hours until the beef is tender.

When the beef is tender, stir in the beurre manié and simmer for 3–4 minutes until the sauce has thickened. Adjust the seasoning, lower the heat and keep warm.

For the macaronade, bring a large pan of well-salted water (1 teaspoon per 600 ml) to the boil. Add the macaroni, stir once and boil for 6–8 minutes or until tender but still *al*

dente. Meanwhile, preheat the grill to high. Drain the macaroni and spoon half into a well-buttered shallow ovenproof dish. Take 250 ml of liquid from the stew, spoon half of it over the macaroni, then sprinkle over half of the cheese. Add the remaining macaroni, enough of the remaining liquid from the stew to moisten, and the cheese. Grill for 3–4 minutes until golden and bubbling. Serve with the stew.

147

This recipe comes from Monsieur Chopolard who has a pork butchery stall at Lavardac market, near Agen. He is very handsome with an elegant moustache and a beret. All his pork comes from his own farm, and it is the combination of his salesmanship with the quality of his pork that keeps the queues in front of his stall long. In this recipe he butchers his loin of pork on the bone so as to be able to slide in slices of Emmenthal cheese and his version of the Italian air-dried ham coppa, which he makes from shoulder of pork and cures until quite dry and hard.

Roast pork with Emmenthal
and air-dried ham *Serves 4–6*

1 x 1.65-kg rack of pork, skinned and chined
150 g Emmenthal cheese, thinly sliced
100 g coppa (about 10 thin slices)

2 tablespoons extra virgin olive oil
Large pinch dried herbes de Provence
200 ml water
100 ml dry white wine

Salt and freshly ground black pepper
Roast potatoes (see page 210), cooked in duck fat, and fine green beans, to serve

Chining the rack of pork detaches the backbone from the ribs, but leaves it still attached to the meat. This makes for easier carving. What you now need to do is to cut pockets into the eye of the meat into which to push the cheese and ham. You can do this from the underside of the joint, cutting between the bones into the meat, or from the fatty side, working down towards the bones. But whichever way you choose, don't cut all the way through and out the opposite side.

Preheat the oven to 230°C/Gas Mark 8. Push the sliced cheese and coppa into each of the pockets and then season the joint lightly with some salt and pepper. Place some sort of rack or trivet into a roasting tin and put the pork on it. Sprinkle over the oil and herbes de Provence, then pour the water into the base of the roasting tin.

Roast the pork for 20 minutes, then lower the oven temperature to 180°C/Gas Mark 4 and continue to cook for 25 minutes per 450 g, i.e. 1 hour and 35 minutes, or until the juices run clear, not pink, when the thickest part of the meat is pierced with a fine skewer.

Lift the pork out of the roasting tin onto a board, cover with foil and leave to rest for 10 minutes. Meanwhile, make the gravy. Remove the trivet and pour the excess fat away from the cooking juices left in the tin. Place the tin directly over a medium-high heat, add the white wine and bring to the boil, rubbing the base of the pan with a wooden spoon to release all the caramelized juices. Leave to simmer to a well-flavoured gravy, adjusting the seasoning if necessary.

Uncover the pork and cut away the backbone. You can either carve the meat between the bones into large, thickish chops, or slice the meat away from the rib bones in one piece and then carve it across into thinner slices. Serve with the gravy and some roast potatoes, cooked in duck fat, and fine green beans.

The key to the success of this simple but exciting dish is the French cider vinegar produced by Maille. I'm a great believer in the superiority of some vinegars over others, and in cider vinegar terms, Maille is one of the best. That and, perhaps surprisingly, being a French-inspired recipe, a little soy sauce too, but the French use it rather more often than you would realize. The famous Chinese cook, the late Kenneth Lo, once said that a lot of Western dishes would be improved by the addition of a little soy sauce. Other than this, there's little to it, except that I've spiked the pork with thin slivers of garlic and accompanied it with a nice bunch of peppery rocket over which you must drizzle a little of the sauce, almost as if dressing a salad.

Pan-fried pork chops with rocket, capers and a cider butter sauce *Serves 4*

4 thick pork loin chops, each weighing about 250 g
1 fat garlic clove
2 tablespoons olive oil
2 tablespoons cider vinegar

1 teaspoon dark soy sauce
25 g chilled butter, cut into small pieces
100 g wild rocket
2 teaspoons nonpareilles capers, drained and rinsed

Salt and freshly ground black pepper
Pommes purée (see page 200), to serve

Preheat the oven to 180°C/Gas Mark 4. Thinly slice the garlic and cut it lengthways into thin slivers. Make a few small, deep incisions into one side of each pork chop and push in some of the garlic, then season them on both sides with salt and pepper.

Heat the olive oil in a large, ovenproof frying pan until smoking hot. Add the chops, lower the heat very slightly and cook them for 2–3 minutes on each side until nicely coloured. Then transfer the pan to the oven and roast them for a further 10 minutes, by which time they should be just cooked through.

Remove the chops from the oven, transfer them to a plate and cover loosely with foil. Turn off the oven and return the chops to the oven to keep warm.

Skim the excess fat from the surface of the pan juices, then place the frying pan back over a high heat and add the cider vinegar and soy sauce, rubbing the base of the pan with a wooden spoon to release all the caramelized juices. Whisk in the pieces of butter, adjust the seasoning if necessary and set to one side.

Divide the rocket between 4 plates and put the pork chops alongside. Spoon the sauce over the pork and a little over the rocket and around the outside edge of the plate, sprinkle over the capers and serve with the puréed potatoes.

I used to cook a rack of lamb à la crème d'ail at our bistro back in the 1990s. The garlic was slow-cooked in the skin, then puréed and mixed with chicken stock and rather a lot of butter and cream. It was nice though a bit overly rich. But I think rack of lamb and the sweet taste of slow-cooked garlic go together so well that here I've mixed crushed new potatoes with nearly two heads of slow-cooked garlic and made a gravy with the residue from cooking the garlic, reduced down with some chicken stock, butter and lemon juice. It's the sort of chunky, earthy flavours of France that I adore.

Roast rack of lamb with crushed potatoes
and slowly caramelized garlic Serves 4

2 x racks of lamb, each weighing about 500 g, trimmed and chined, and the chine bone removed
Salt and freshly ground black pepper

FOR THE CRUSHED POTATOES WITH SLOWLY CARAMELIZED GARLIC:
2 x 75–80-g heads garlic
25 g butter
1 tablespoon olive oil
100 ml *Chicken stock* (see page 208)
750 g new potatoes, scraped clean
15 g chopped flat-leaf parsley

FOR THE GARLIC GRAVY:
50 ml *Chicken stock* (see page 208)
$\frac{1}{2}$ teaspoon lemon juice
10 g butter

Preheat the oven to 230°C/Gas Mark 8. For the slowly caramelized garlic, peel the cloves from each of the 2 heads and put them into a small pan with the butter and olive oil. Sauté gently until just starting to colour, then add the chicken stock, press a sheet of crumpled wet greaseproof paper down onto the top of them and leave to cook very gently for 15 minutes.

Meanwhile, put the potatoes into a pan of well-salted water (1 teaspoon per 600 ml), bring to the boil and simmer for 15–20 minutes until tender. Season the racks of lamb with salt and pepper, put them into a small roasting tin and roast for 25 minutes. Remove the lamb from the oven, cover tightly with some foil and leave somewhere warm to rest for up to 10 minutes.

Lift the soft, caramelized garlic out of its cooking juices onto a board and coarsely chop. Drain the potatoes well, return them to the pan and gently crush each one up against the side of the pan with the back of a fork until it just bursts open. Add two-thirds of the garlic, the chopped parsley and a little seasoning and lightly mix them together.

For the garlic gravy, return the pan of garlic cooking juices to a high heat, add the chicken stock, lemon juice and remaining chopped caramelized garlic and boil rapidly until reduced slightly and well flavoured. Whisk in the butter and season to taste with some salt and pepper.

Carve the racks of lamb into cutlets. Spoon the crushed potatoes into the centre of 4 warmed plates and rest the cutlets alongside. Spoon around the garlic gravy and serve.

The trick with all stuffings is to vary them according to the texture and richness of the meat to be stuffed. A boned and rolled loin of lamb stuffed with kidneys is rich and pleasantly fatty and so doesn't suit a lot of strongly flavoured stuffing. You should go for a bland stuffing, such as sage and onion, or in this case a small amount of a fresh spinach and herb paste, which perfectly complements the moist pinkness of the lamb and kidneys. This is the sort of joint that you would find ready prepared in a very smart French boucherie.

Roast loin of lamb stuffed with kidneys, spinach, mustard and lemon *Serves 6*

1 tablespoon olive oil
120 g spinach leaves, washed and dried
20 g flat-leaf parsley leaves, chopped
2 teaspoons Dijon mustard
2 teaspoons lemon juice

2 boned loins of lamb, each weighing about 500 g, with the flank still attached
4 large fresh lamb's kidneys
100 ml red wine
150 ml *Chicken stock* (see page 208)

1 teaspoon *Beurre manié* (see page 210)
Salt and freshly ground black pepper
Pommes dauphinoise (see page 202) and *Melange of baby spring vegetables* (see page 204), to serve

Gently heat the olive oil in a small pan. Add the spinach leaves and as soon as they have wilted down, tip into a small sieve and press out as much of the excess liquid as you can. Transfer to a mini food processor and add the chopped parsley, mustard and lemon juice along with ½ teaspoon of salt and some black pepper. Blend to a smooth paste.

Put the prepared loins of lamb onto a board, skin-side down, and open them out. Season the meat well with salt and pepper, then spread half of the spinach mixture down the centre of each one. Remove any membrane from the kidneys and snip out the cores with kitchen scissors, leaving them whole. Lay 2 kidneys in a line down the centre of each loin and sprinkle with a little more salt and pepper. Wrap the lamb round the kidneys and tie along the length of each one at 3–4 cm intervals with string to make 2 neat, cylindrical joints. Weigh them and calculate the cooking time, allowing 16 minutes per 450 g.

Preheat the oven to 230°C/Gas Mark 8. Season the lamb with salt and pepper, put into a small roasting tin and roast for 15 minutes, then lower the oven temperature to 200°C/Gas Mark 6 and continue to roast for the remainder of the calculated cooking time – approximately 24 minutes. Remove from the oven, cover with foil and leave to rest for at least 10 minutes.

Meanwhile, make the gravy. Pour the excess fat away from the tin, place it over a medium-high heat and add the red wine. Bring to the boil, rubbing the base of the pan to release all the caramelized juices, and reduce down to 2 tablespoons. Add the chicken stock, strain into a small pan and boil once more until reduced to a well-flavoured gravy. Whisk in the beurre manié and leave to simmer for 2–3 minutes. Carve each loin across into 6 slices and serve with the gravy, pommes dauphinoise and baby spring vegetables.

Roast loin of veal with Madeira sauce
and creamed spinach *Serves 8–10*

1 x 4.5-kg loin of veal, French trimmed
4 tablespoons olive oil
2 medium onions, halved and sliced
250 g peeled carrots, sliced
250 g celery, sliced
4 sprigs of thyme
6 bay leaves
Salt and freshly ground black pepper

FOR THE MADEIRA SAUCE:
2 tablespoons plain flour
1 teaspoon tomato purée
75 ml Madeira
1 litre *Chicken stock* (see page 208)

FOR THE CREAMED SPINACH:
25 g butter

2 kg spinach, large stalks removed, washed
150 ml double cream
Freshly grated nutmeg

2 quantities of *Pommes Anna* (see page 201), to serve

Preheat the oven to 230°C/Gas Mark 8. Weigh the loin of veal and if it's not exactly 4.5 kg then calculate the cooking time, allowing 15 minutes per 500 g. This will give you veal cooked to medium – just pink in the middle. Then rub the joint with a little of the olive oil and season well with salt and pepper. Now you need to protect the piece of fillet that runs along one side of the joint. This is a more tender piece of meat and will take less time to cook than the rest of the joint. Tie the joint along its length with string into a neat shape, folding over the top flap of meat so that it partially covers the exposed fillet, then take a double thickness length of foil and wrap it closely round the part of the fillet not already covered by the top flap of meat.

Put the rest of the oil into a large roasting tin, add the onions, carrots, celery, thyme and bay leaves, and toss together until well coated. Push them to the outside edges of the tin and put the joint of veal into the centre, bone-side down, fat-side up. Put into the oven and roast for 40 minutes. Then lower the oven temperature to 180°C/Gas Mark 4 and continue to roast for 1 hour 40 minutes. The core temperature of the joint should be about 57°C when it comes out of the oven, continuing to rise to 60°C as it rests.

Lift the veal onto a board and cover tightly with foil and leave somewhere warm to rest for anything up to 30 minutes. Meanwhile, make the Madeira sauce. Pour away the excess

fat from the roasting tin and place it over a medium-high heat. Stir in the flour and cook until pale nutty brown in colour, then add the tomato purée and Madeira and bring to the boil, rubbing the base of the tin with a wooden spoon to release all the caramelized juices. Stir in the chicken stock and then transfer everything to a saucepan and leave to simmer for 10–15 minutes to extract the flavour from the vegetables. Then strain through a fine sieve into a clean pan, leave it to settle and spoon off the excess fat from the surface again. Increase the heat and simmer rapidly until reduced to a well-flavoured gravy. Season to taste and keep warm.

For the creamed spinach, melt the butter in a large pan. Add the spinach, a large handful at a time, until it has all wilted down into the bottom of the pan. Cook over a high heat for 1 minute, then tip into a colander and press out the excess liquid. Transfer to a chopping board and pass a knife once or twice through the leaves to coarsely chop. Return to the pan, add the cream and season to taste with grated nutmeg, salt and pepper. Reheat gently and keep warm.

Remove the foil and string from the veal and then slice the fillet and the main piece of meat away from either side of the bones in one piece. Discard the bones, carve the meat across into thin slices and transfer to a warmed serving plate. Pour the Madeira sauce into a gravy boat, and take the meat and gravy to the table with the creamed spinach and pommes Anna.

Plane trees reflected in the Canal du Midi as it nears the Mediterranean

155

My first experience of eating a Moroccan tagine was in Paris in the early seventies. The tagine arrived with fourteen sparklers stuck into a big pile of couscous and my lasting memory of a very indifferent dish is the smell of gunpowder. A subsequent trip to Morocco didn't do anything to improve my enthusiasm. It was only when I started frequenting North African restaurants in the south of France that I suddenly realized what a wonderfully aromatic way of stewing meat a tagine is. And nor do you have to use the pot of the same name – a shallow, heatproof clay dish with a tall conical lid – for cooking this dish. The ras el hanout we used is available mail order from www.seasonedpioneers.co.uk. What I love about their mix is the dried rose petals it has in it.

Moroccan lamb tagine with ras el hanout
and couscous *Serves 4–6*

2 kg lamb shanks, cut across into
   slices about 4 cm thick

3 tablespoons olive oil

4 teaspoons ras el hanout (see above)

450 g carrots, peeled and cut on the
   diagonal into 7.5-cm pieces

200 g onions, sliced

8 x 50-g waxy potatoes, such as
   Charlotte, peeled

400 g sweet potatoes, peeled and
   cut into pieces the same size as the
   potatoes

450 g vine-ripened tomatoes, thickly
   sliced

75 g dried apricots (not no-need-to-
   soak)

2 tablespoons clear honey

1.2 litres *Chicken stock* (see page 208)

3 bay leaves

Salt and freshly ground black pepper

FOR THE SPICE PASTE:

4 garlic cloves

2 shallots, roughly chopped

1 red chilli, seeded and roughly
   chopped

Stalks from a 20-g packet fresh
   coriander, leaves reserved

1 teaspoon freshly ground white
   pepper

1/2 teaspoon salt

FOR THE BUTTERED COUSCOUS:

450 g couscous

1/2 teaspoon salt

450 ml boiling water

25 g butter

2 tablespoons olive oil

Trim the lamb of any excess fat and then season well with salt and pepper.

For the spice paste, put all the ingredients into a mini-food processor – or use a mortar and pestle – and grind to a smooth paste.

Heat the olive oil in a large flameproof casserole. Add the lamb pieces and brown on both sides. Lift onto a plate and set aside.

Add the spice paste to the remaining oil left in the casserole and fry gently for 2–3 minutes. Add the ras el hanout and fry for a further minute. Add the carrots, onions, potatoes and sweet potatoes, tomatoes and apricots and turn over a few times in the spice mixture. Return the lamb to the pan and add the honey and enough stock to not

Spice market in Marseille

quite cover the meat. Add the bay leaves and 1 teaspoon of salt, bring to the boil and leave to simmer gently, uncovered, for 1½–2 hours, turning the pieces of meat every now and then as the liquid reduces, until the lamb is tender.

Ten minutes before the tagine is cooked, put the couscous and salt into a large bowl and stir in the boiling water. Cover with a tea towel and leave to soak for 5 minutes. Then uncover and fluff up into separate grains with a fork. Melt the butter with the oil in a large pan, add the couscous and stir over a low heat for a couple of minutes until heated through.

Skim the excess oil from the top of the stew. Chop the remaining coriander leaves, scatter over the top, and serve at the table from the casserole, with the couscous.

I've written this recipe for only two people because it's one of those dishes where seconds count and cooking for four may well result in overcooked liver. You need to have everything to hand before you start, and it will all be ready in less than five minutes.

Calf's liver with parsley, sage and mushrooms

Serves 2

350 g thinly sliced calf's or lamb's liver
Plain flour for dusting
25 g butter
1 teaspoon olive oil
100 g Portobello or chestnut mushrooms, wiped clean and chopped

1 garlic clove, finely chopped
1 teaspoon finely chopped sage
1 teaspoon chopped chives
1 teaspoon finely chopped parsley, plus extra to garnish
Salt and freshly ground black pepper

¹/₂ quantity *Sautéed potatoes* (see page 201) and *Green lettuce salad with Orléanais dressing* (see page 205), to serve

Season the liver on both sides with some salt and pepper, dust lightly with the flour and then shake off the excess.

Heat a small knob of the butter and the oil in a large frying pan – about 30 cm across – until quite hot. Add half of the liver slices and sear quickly for 30 seconds on each side. Lift onto a plate. Add another small knob of butter to the pan, followed by the rest of the liver, and sear quickly for another 30 seconds on each side. Set the liver aside.

Add the rest of the butter to the pan, followed by the mushrooms, garlic, herbs and some salt and pepper. Fry over a medium-high heat for 2 minutes, then return the liver to the pan and toss everything together very briefly – you don't want the liver to cook any further.

Transfer the liver to warmed serving plates, scatter with a little more chopped parsley and serve with the sautéed potatoes and salad.

Morning mist in late September near Agen

As with the calf's liver recipe on the facing page, this dish is cooked extremely quickly, so it's important to make sure that you have all the ingredients ready and to hand before you start.

Sautéed lamb's kidneys on toasted brioche
with Sauvignon Blanc, mustard and tarragon *Serves 4*

750 g lamb's kidneys
50 g unsalted butter
150 ml dry white wine, such as
 Sauvignon Blanc
1 tablespoon Dijon mustard
4 teaspoons chopped fresh tarragon

4 tablespoons double cream
4 x 2-cm-thick slices brioche taken from
 a loaf
Salt and freshly ground black pepper
Sprigs of tarragon, to garnish

Cut each kidney in half lengthways and snip out the white cores with kitchen scissors. Season lightly with salt and pepper.

Melt half the butter in a large frying pan. Add half the kidneys and fry over a high heat for 1½–2 minutes on each side until lightly browned and just firm but still pink and juicy in the centre. Lift out with a slotted spoon onto a plate and repeat with the rest of the butter and the kidneys. Cover and keep hot.

Add the wine to the pan with any juices from the plate of kidneys and boil until reduced slightly, to about 8 tablespoons. Add the mustard, chopped tarragon and cream and continue to boil for a minute or two longer until reduced to a good sauce consistency. Season to taste with salt and pepper.

Meanwhile, toast the brioche and cut each slice in half. Overlap 2 pieces on each of 4 warmed plates and top with the kidneys. Spoon over the sauce and serve garnished with the tarragon sprigs.

Escalopes of pork with a crisp fennel and green bean salad *Serves 4*

1 large pork fillet, weighing about
  450–500 g
45 g plain flour
2 medium eggs, beaten
225 g fresh white breadcrumbs or 150 g
  Japanese panko crumbs
Sunflower oil, for shallow frying
Salt and freshly ground black pepper
Lemon wedges, to garnish

FOR THE FENNEL AND GREEN BEAN SALAD:
2 bulbs fennel, each about 200 g
150 g fine green beans
2 tablespoons extra virgin olive oil
2$^{1}/_{2}$ teaspoons lemon juice
Leaves from 20 g flat-leaf parsley,
  chopped
30 g thinly shaved Parmesan cheese

First prepare the escalopes from the fillet. Starting at the thinner end of the fillet, slice the meat very sharply on the diagonal (much as you would smoked salmon) into eight 50–60-g slices. Then put each slice in turn between 2 sheets of clingfilm and flatten slightly with a rolling pin into a piece about the size of a small saucer.

For the salad, trim the fennel, remove and discard the outside layer if damaged and then thinly slice it lengthways through the root on a mandolin. Cut the green beans in half lengthways, drop them into a pan of well-salted boiling water (1 teaspoon per 600 ml) and cook for 3–4 minutes until just tender. Drain and refresh under cold water. For the dressing, whisk the olive oil and lemon juice together with some salt and pepper to taste.

Season the escalopes on both sides with salt and pepper. Dip in the flour and pat off the excess, then dip into the beaten egg, and finally the breadcrumbs, pressing them on well to give an even coating. Lay out on a baking tray, separated by a sheet of clingfilm if necessary.

Pour 1 cm of sunflower oil into a large frying pan and heat it to 190°C. Add 4 of the escalopes and fry for 1 minute on each side until crisp and golden. Transfer to a tray lined with kitchen paper and keep hot in a low oven. Repeat with the remaining escalopes.

Toss the fennel, beans and parsley with the lemon dressing and adjust the seasoning if necessary. Divide between 4 plates and scatter with the Parmesan cheese shavings. Rest the escalopes partly on top of the salad, garnish with lemon wedges and serve.

The great thing about fillet steak is it's always beautifully tender, but it can also be a bit bland. While I was on the barge we went to a catering supermarket, the like of which I've never seen in the UK, where you could buy not only whole fillets of beef, whole foie gras and cases of magret de canard, but also everything you need to run a restaurant. Tables, chairs, commercial cookers, ice machines, wine, barrels of beer – the lot. All the food was of first-class quality and I came back with a whole fillet of beef, which only cost half what I would have had to pay elsewhere. I simply brushed it with olive oil, seasoned it and roasted it in the oven, and served it up with some enormous, misshapen Provençal tomatoes which I'd stuffed with lots of garlic, parsley and anchovy breadcrumbs, a salad and some frites. I've cooked it a few times since then and I think the fillet is improved by heavy seasoning with cracked black pepper and plenty of sea salt flakes and then being seared on the top of the stove before roasting.

Roast fillet of beef with Provençal tomatoes

Serves 6

A piece of beef fillet, cut from the
   centre of a whole fillet, weighing
   about 1.5 kg
Olive oil for brushing
Salt and freshly ground black pepper
Sprigs of flat-leaf parsley to garnish

FOR THE PROVENÇAL TOMATOES:
3 large Marmande or beef tomatoes
4 garlic cloves, finely chopped
6 anchovy fillets in olive oil, drained
   and chopped
15 g flat-leaf parsley leaves, chopped
1/2 teaspoon dried mixed herbes de
   Provence

Pinch crushed dried chillies
40 g white breadcrumbs, made from
   1- or 2-day-old bread
2 tablespoons extra virgin olive oil

Pommes frites (see page 200) and
   *Green lettuce salad with Orléanais
   dressing* (see page 205), to serve

Preheat the oven to 200°C/Gas Mark 6. Cut the tomatoes in half and loosen as many of the seeds as you can with a fingertip, then turn the tomatoes upside down and give each half a shake to remove most of the seeds and make little cavities for the stuffing. Season the cut face of each tomato half with 1/4 teaspoon of salt and plenty of black pepper and place cut-side up in a small, oiled roasting tin. Mix the chopped garlic, anchovies, parsley, dried herbes de Provence, dried chillies, breadcrumbs, 1/2 teaspoon salt and some black pepper together in a bowl. Sprinkle some of the breadcrumb stuffing over each tomato, gently pressing some of it down into the cavities, then add a little more to completely cover the surface. Drizzle 1 teaspoon of oil over each tomato.

Rub the piece of beef fillet with olive oil and season very well with plenty of salt and plenty of freshly ground black pepper. Heat an ovenproof frying pan over a high heat and, when smoking hot, add the beef and sear for 2 minutes on either side until nicely browned. Transfer to the oven with the tomatoes and roast for 15–20 minutes.

Remove the beef from the oven, but leave the tomatoes for another 5 minutes or so until they are tender and the topping is crisp and golden. Cover the beef tightly with foil and leave to rest somewhere warm.

To serve, lift the beef onto a board and carve across into thin slices. Divide between 6 warmed plates, place half a tomato alongside and drizzle with the juices from both the beef and the tomatoes. Garnish with sprigs of flat-leaf parsley and serve with the frites and green salad.

The steak is cooked rare and served with a long-cooked sauce made of shin of beef, pig's trotter, wild mushrooms, red wine, garlic and thyme, finished with a gremolata of garlic, orange zest and parsley.

Pan-fried fillet steak
with the slow-cooked flavours of daube *Serves 4*

4 x 175–200-g fillet steaks, cut 4 cm
  thick
15 g unsalted butter
Salt and freshly ground black pepper

FOR THE STOCK:
4 tablespoons sunflower oil
750 g shin of beef on the bone
25 g butter
2 carrots, roughly chopped
1 medium onion, roughly chopped
$\frac{1}{2}$ celery stick, roughly chopped
2 garlic cloves, sliced

$1\frac{1}{2}$ teaspoons tomato purée
300 ml red wine, such as a Cabernet
  Sauvignon
1 tablespoon brandy
1 pig's trotter
7 g dried porcini mushrooms
1 fresh bay leaf
1 sprig of thyme
1 pared strip of orange peel
5 black peppercorns

FOR THE GARNISH:
40 g butter
12 unpeeled garlic cloves
16 button mushrooms, halved

FOR THE GREMOLATA:
1 pared strip of orange peel, very
  finely chopped
1 small garlic clove, finely chopped
1 tablespoon chopped flat-leaf parsley

Celeriac and potato mash (see page
  200), to serve

For the stock, heat the oil in a large, heavy-based pan, add the beef shin and fry until well coloured. Remove from the pan, add the butter, vegetables and garlic and fry until nicely browned. Stir in the tomato purée and cook for 2 minutes. Return the beef to the pan and add the red wine, brandy, pig's trotter, dried porcini, herbs, orange peel, peppercorns and 1.75 litres water. Bring to the boil, skim off any scum and leave to simmer for 4 hours. Then strain the stock into a clean, shallow pan (reserve the pig's trotter) and boil rapidly until reduced to about 300 ml. Meanwhile, remove the meat from the pig's trotter, cut it into fine shreds, cover and set aside.

While the stock is reducing, prepare the garnish. Melt 15 g of the butter in a small pan, add the unpeeled cloves of garlic, and fry until golden. Add 2 tablespoons of the stock, cover and simmer for 10 minutes until tender. Melt another 15 g butter in another small pan, add the mushrooms and fry until lightly browned. Season and set aside.

Season the pieces of steak on each side with salt and pepper. Heat a heavy-based frying pan until smoking hot, lower the temperature slightly, add the butter and the steaks and cook for 3 minutes on each side until cooked to rare. While the steak is cooking, whisk the remaining 2 teaspoons of butter into the reduced sauce. Stir in the garlic cloves, mushrooms and pig's trotter and keep warm. Mix together the ingredients for the gremolata. To serve, put the steaks onto 4 warm plates and spoon over some of the sauce. Garnish with the garlic cloves and mushrooms, sprinkle over the gremolata and serve with the celeriac and potato mash.

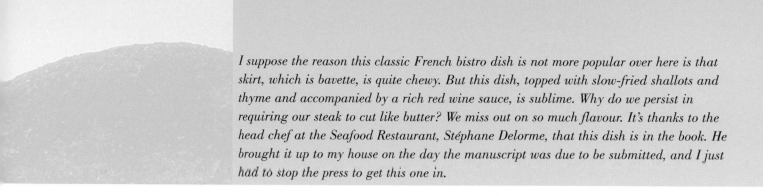

I suppose the reason this classic French bistro dish is not more popular over here is that skirt, which is bavette, is quite chewy. But this dish, topped with slow-fried shallots and thyme and accompanied by a rich red wine sauce, is sublime. Why do we persist in requiring our steak to cut like butter? We miss out on so much flavour. It's thanks to the head chef at the Seafood Restaurant, Stéphane Delorme, that this dish is in the book. He brought it up to my house on the day the manuscript was due to be submitted, and I just had to stop the press to get this one in.

Bavette bordelaise with pommes Coq d'Or
and cheesemaker's salad *Serves 4*

4 x 225-g long, thin pieces of beef skirt
2 tablespoons sunflower oil
Salt and freshly ground black pepper

Pommes Coq d'Or (see page 201) and
 Patricia Wells's cheesemaker's salad
 (see page 206), to serve

FOR THE BORDELAISE SAUCE:
40 g unsalted butter
1 garlic clove, finely chopped
1 shallot, finely chopped
200 ml good quality red wine, such
 as Bordeaux
600 ml *Beef stock*, browned (see
 page 208)

**FOR THE SHALLOT AND THYME
GARNISH:**
4 tablespoons sunflower oil
750 g shallots, peeled and very thinly
 sliced
45 g unsalted butter
1 tablespoon thyme leaves

For the bordelaise sauce, melt 15 g of butter in a small pan, add the garlic and shallot and sauté gently until soft and very lightly browned. Add the red wine and simmer rapidly until reduced by three-quarters. Add the beef stock and continue to simmer rapidly until reduced once more by three-quarters.

Meanwhile, for the shallot and thyme garnish, heat the sunflower oil in a large shallow pan, add the shallots and sauté until they are soft and lightly caramelized. Add the butter and thyme leaves and continue to sauté until richly browned and almost crispy. Set aside and keep warm.

Pass the bordelaise sauce through a fine sieve into a clean pan, bring back to a simmer and whisk in the remaining butter a small piece at a time. Season to taste and keep warm.

Season the bavettes with salt and pepper. Heat a large frying pan until hot, add the sunflower oil and the bavettes and fry them for 2 minutes on each side until nicely browned.

To serve, spoon some of the bordelaise sauce onto each plate and place a bavette on top. Spoon a quarter of the shallot and thyme garnish along each one and serve with the pommes Coq d'Or and cheesemaker's salad.

A farmer on his way to market

I'm continually beguiled by the idea of cooking steaks over a wood fire. I love the restaurant in Bordeaux called La Tupina simply because all the côtes de boeuf, sirloin and rump steaks are grilled on a wood fire set in a vast open hearth. They not only cook steaks there, they also roast joints and game on rotating spits driven by clockwork-motor weights and pulleys, which would give a skip to any boy's heart. They also fry chips in duck fat on little gridirons set above the main fire, and the aroma and spectacle of it are a joy. This is the 'why' of this dish, rump steaks cooked over a wood fire. You cook the steaks once the flames have subsided and you have a glowing pile of red and grey embers. Garlic butter is the perfect embellishment.

Rib-eye steaks cooked over an open fire
with garlic butter and goose-fat chips *Serves 4*

4 x 225–250-g ribeye steaks
A little olive oil
Sea salt and freshly ground black
 pepper

FOR THE GARLIC BUTTER:
2 large garlic cloves
100 g unsalted butter, at room
 temperature
1 teaspoon lemon juice

25 g chopped parsley

Radicchio and oakleaf salad with
 ***sherry vinegar dressing* (see page**
 206), to serve

For the garlic butter, crush the garlic cloves on a board under the blade of a large kitchen knife. Add a large pinch of salt and work into a smooth paste, using the side of the knife blade. Scrape the paste into a bowl and add the butter, lemon juice, parsley, another $1/4$ teaspoon salt and some black pepper. Mix together well and then spoon onto a sheet of clingfilm and shape into a log about 3 cm thick. Wrap in more clingfilm and chill or freeze until needed.

Light a fire using plenty of wood, outside or in your hearth if you have one. Allow the fire to get good and hot and then leave it until the flames have died down and you are left with a thick bed of glowing embers.

Meanwhile, prepare some sort of rack on which to cook your steaks – a proper rack on legs designed specifically for the purpose or some sort of hinged wire rack for using over charcoal barbecues. You want the steaks to be about 13 cm above the embers when you come to cook them. Cook the chips according to the instructions on page 200 up to the first deep-frying stage.

Brush the steaks with olive oil and season with sea salt and freshly ground black pepper. Place the rack over the fire and cook the steaks for 2 minutes on each side for rare, $2^1/2$ for medium-rare and 3 minutes on each side for medium.

Transfer the steaks to warmed plates, then drop the chips back into the fat and fry for another 1–2 minutes until crisp and golden. Drain well on lots of kitchen paper and sprinkle lightly with salt. Take 8 slices of garlic butter from the roll, put 2 slices on top of each steak, and serve straight away with the chips and salad.

Desserts

One of the great delights of French cuisine is the puddings, and I don't mean the over-elaborate stuff you get in starred restaurants – seven different ways with chocolate on one plate, that sort of thing. This deep baked cheesecake is particularly irresistible because it incorporates the digestive biscuit base of American cheesecakes and therefore features the best of both cuisines.

Baked lemon cheesecake
with summer berry compote *Serves 10–12*

FOR THE BASE:
100 g butter, plus extra for greasing
200 g digestive biscuits
2 tablespoons caster or demerara sugar

FOR THE FILLING:
500 g full-fat cream cheese
200 g caster sugar
3 medium eggs
2 tablespoons cornflour
300 ml crème fraîche
Finely grated zest of 1 lemon and 3 tablespoons juice

FOR THE SUMMER BERRY COMPOTE:
225 g raspberries
50 g caster sugar
Finely grated zest of $1/2$ orange
350 g mixed summer berries (halved small strawberries, raspberries and blueberries)

Icing sugar, to serve

Lightly butter a 20-cm clip-sided tin and base line with a piece of non-stick baking parchment or buttered greaseproof paper. Preheat the oven to 150°C/Gas Mark 2.

Melt the butter in a pan over a low heat. Crush the biscuits into crumbs in a plastic bag, add to the butter along with the sugar and mix together well. Tip into the tin, level out and press onto the base in an even layer with the back of a spoon. Set aside.

Beat the cream cheese and sugar together in a bowl until smooth. Add the eggs, one at a time, and beat well between each addition. Add the cornflour, crème fraîche, lemon zest and juice and beat once more.

Pour the mixture onto the base and bake in the centre of the oven for 50 minutes to 1 hour, or until just set but with still a slight wobble in the centre. Now turn off the oven but leave the cheesecake inside, and let it go cold.

For the summer berry compote, put the raspberries, sugar and orange zest into a bowl and crush with the back of a fork into a purée. Rub through a sieve into a clean bowl and stir in the summer berries. Chill until you are ready to serve.

To serve, carefully remove the cheesecake from its tin – you might need to run a round-bladed knife around the edge first – and transfer it to a serving plate. Dust the top with a little icing sugar and serve, cut into wedges, with the summer berry compote.

Previous page: Poplar trees, used for drainage and wind protection all across France

The points to note in making tarte tatin are (a) the apples – I go for Cox's in most apple dishes; you need a firm eating apple that will not easily fall apart – and (b) the making of the caramel. It needs to be done over a medium heat, taking your time to allow the butter, sugar and apple juices to reach a nice toffee colour before topping the dish with the puff pastry and baking it. I think crème fraîche or vanilla ice cream make the perfect accompaniments. One of the best puddings in the world.

Tarte tatin *Serves 6*

250 g puff pastry
75 g softened butter
175 g caster sugar
750 g (about 5) large firm dessert apples,
  such as Cox's

Vanilla ice cream (see page 207) or crème
  fraîche, to serve

Roll out the pastry on a lightly floured surface and cut out a 26-cm disc, slightly larger than the top of a 20-cm tarte tatin dish or reliably non-stick cast-iron frying pan. Transfer to a baking sheet and chill for at least 20 minutes.

Spread the butter over the base of the tarte tatin dish or frying pan, and sprinkle over the sugar in a thick, even layer.

Peel, core and halve the apples, trimming them very slightly if necessary to fit but keeping their nicely rounded shape, and then tightly pack them, rounded-side down, on top of the sugar. Place the tarte tatin dish or frying pan over a medium heat and cook for 20–25 minutes, gently shaking the pan now and then, until the butter and sugar have amalgamated with the apple juices to produce a rich toffee-coloured sauce and the apples are just tender. At first the caramel will be pale and liquid from the juices from the apples, but as you keep on cooking the juices will evaporate and the butter and sugar will become darker and thicker. Just take care that the butter and sugar are not allowed to burn.

Preheat the oven to 190°C/Gas Mark 5. Lift the pastry on top of the apples and tuck the edges down inside the pan. Prick the pastry 5 or 6 times with the tip of a small, sharp knife, transfer to the oven and bake for 25 minutes until the pastry is puffed up, crisp and golden.

Remove the tart from the oven and leave it to rest for 5 minutes. Then run a knife round the edge of the tart and invert it onto a round, flat serving plate. Serve warm, cut into wedges, with crème fraîche or vanilla ice cream.

Prune and almond tart with Armagnac

Serves 8

300 g dried or mi-cuit Agen prunes
4 tablespoons Armagnac
1 quantity *Rich shortcrust pastry* (see page 211), and butter for greasing
1 large egg, lightly beaten
35 g ground almonds

55 g caster sugar
1 x 200-ml tub crème fraîche
Icing sugar, for dusting
Extra crème fraîche, to serve

Put the prunes into a small bowl, pour over the Armagnac and leave for 1 hour, turning them over every now and then to help them soak up the alcohol.

Roll out the pastry on a lightly floured surface and use to line a greased loose-bottomed flan tin that is 2.5 cm deep and 25 cm across the base. Prick the base here and there with a fork and chill for 20 minutes.

Preheat the oven to 200°C/Gas Mark 6. Line the pastry case with a crumpled sheet of greaseproof paper and a thin layer of baking beans and bake for 15 minutes. Remove the paper and beans and return to the oven for 4–5 minutes. Remove, brush the inside of the case with a little of the beaten egg and return to the oven once more for 2 minutes. Set aside and lower the oven temperature to 190°C/Gas Mark 5.

Drain the prunes over a bowl to reserve the Armagnac. Add the ground almonds, egg, sugar and crème fraîche to the Armagnac, and beat together until smooth. Scatter the prunes over the base of the pastry case, pour over the almond mixture and bake for 45 minutes until golden brown and a skewer pushed into the centre of the tart comes away clean.

Carefully remove the tart from the tin and leave to cool slightly on a wire rack. Dust with a little icing sugar and serve warm or at room temperature, cut into wedges, with some more crème fraîche.

I wanted to slip a mussel dish called éclade into the book, which we filmed for the series on the Anse de l'Aiguillon just above La Rochelle. You take a sheet of steel and arrange the mussels on it in a vast disc, all lying hinge-side up. Copious quantities of pine needles are sprinkled over the top, set alight and allowed to burn down, by which time the mussels are cooked and have a wonderful, pinewood-smoke flavour. They are then consumed with one or two bottles of ice-cold Muscadet or any white wine from the Charente. You can imagine that this is not really practical as a recipe, although we did try it once in Trevone, many books ago. But the other great dish of this long stretch of beach fringed by pine forests is the pine kernel tart. It's just the sort of unusual goût de terroir dish I love: pine kernels and eau de vie-soaked sultanas set in an almond paste.

Tarte aux pignons
Pine nut tart *Serves 8–10*

50 g sultanas

2 tablespoons clear eau de vie, such as kirsch or grappa

1 quantity *Sweet pastry* (see page 211)

100 g butter, softened, plus extra for greasing

50 g caster sugar

2 medium eggs

50 g ground almonds

100 g pine nuts

Icing sugar, to dust

Whipped cream or crème fraîche, to serve (optional)

Mix the sultanas and eau de vie together in a small bowl and leave to soak for 2 hours, turning them over now and then.

Roll out the pastry thinly on a lightly floured surface and use to line a loose-bottomed flan tin that is 2.5 cm deep and 22 cm across the base. Prick the base here and there with a fork and chill for 20–30 minutes.

Preheat the oven to 200°C/Gas Mark 6. Line the pastry case with crumpled greaseproof paper, cover the base with a thin layer of baking beans and bake for 12–15 minutes until the edges are biscuit-coloured. Carefully remove the paper and beans and return the pastry case to the oven for 3–4 minutes, until golden. Remove and lower the oven temperature to 180°C/Gas Mark 4.

For the filling, put the butter into a bowl and beat until very soft. Add the sugar and beat until light and fluffy, beat in the eggs one at a time, adding a few of the ground almonds with the second egg to prevent the mixture from curdling. Mix in the rest of the ground almonds and any eau de vie that hasn't been absorbed by the sultanas. Fold in the sultanas and 75 g of the pine nuts and spread the mixture evenly over the base of the pastry case. Scatter the rest of the pine nuts over the top and bake for 15 minutes, or until nicely golden. Cover loosely with a sheet of foil (dome it slightly so that it doesn't touch the top of the tart) and continue to cook for 10–15 minutes until a skewer, inserted into the centre of the almond mixture, comes away clean. Remove and leave to cool.

When cold, remove the tart from the tin, dust lightly with icing sugar and serve cut into wedges, with a little whipped cream or crème fraîche if you wish.

Hazelnut and chocolate dacquoise

Serves 8–10

FOR THE HAZELNUT MERINGUE:
50 g shelled hazelnuts
4 large, very fresh egg whites
225 g caster sugar

FOR THE CHOCOLATE CREAM:
100 g plain chocolate, with only 50% cocoa solids
150 ml crème fraîche
150 ml double cream

Icing sugar, for dusting
Pouring cream, to serve

Preheat the oven to 200°C/Gas Mark 6. Spread the hazelnuts onto a baking sheet and roast for 5–6 minutes until golden brown. If they were unblanched, put them into a tea towel and rub off their papery skins. Leave to cool and then very finely chop. Lower the oven temperature to 110°C/Gas Mark ¼.

Line 3 baking sheets with non-stick baking parchment and mark each one with a 20-cm circle. In a large bowl, whisk the egg whites into stiff peaks. Gradually whisk in the sugar to make a stiff, glossy meringue, then fold in all but 1 tablespoon of the chopped hazelnuts.

Divide the meringue equally between each of the baking sheets and spread the mixture out within the marked circles to make 3 discs. Sprinkle one disc with the rest of the chopped nuts. Bake for 2 hours, then turn off the oven and leave them to go cold inside.

Fill the dacquoise no more than 2 hours before serving. For the chocolate cream, break the chocolate into a heatproof bowl and rest it over a pan of just simmering water. Leave to melt, then add the crème fraîche and stir gently until smooth and glossy, then remove the bowl from the heat. Whip the double cream in a small bowl until just beginning to thicken and gently fold in. You want to achieve a mixture that is smooth and glossy and just holding its shape.

Put one of the plain discs onto a flat serving plate and spread with half of the chocolate mixture. Cover with the second plain meringue disc and spread with the rest of the chocolate mixture. Cover with the last nut-covered disc and chill in the fridge for 2 hours, to allow time for the filling to set and the meringue layers to soften slightly.

To serve, dust the top lightly with icing sugar and cut into thin wedges with a sharp (serrated) knife. Serve with pouring cream.

Crunchy walnut tart
with chestnut honey *Serves 8–10*

120 g unsalted butter
150 g chestnut honey
100 ml double cream
2 tablespoons rum
300 g walnut pieces
150 g caster sugar
5 egg yolks

FOR THE PASTRY:
180 g unsalted butter, plus extra
  for greasing
240 g plain flour
Pinch of salt
2–3 tablespoons cold water

Crème fraîche, to serve

Remove the butter from the fridge 30 minutes before making the pastry. Sift the flour and salt onto a work surface. Cut the butter into smallish pieces, add to the flour and lightly rub together to partly combine. Make a well in the centre, add the water and, using a pastry scraper, work the paste to a rough heap of buttery lumps of dough. Then work together as briefly as possible into a smooth dough, roll out on a lightly floured surface and use to line a loose-bottomed flan tin that is 2.5 cm deep and 24 cm across the base. Prick the base here and there with a fork and chill for 20 minutes.

Preheat the oven to 200°C/Gas Mark 6. Line the pastry case with a sheet of crumpled greaseproof paper and a thin layer of baking beans and bake for 20 minutes. Remove the paper and beans and return to the oven for 10 minutes. Remove and lower the oven temperature to 190°C/Gas Mark 5.

Put the butter, honey, cream and rum together in a saucepan and warm gently over a low heat, but don't let it get hot. Mix the walnuts and sugar together in a bowl. Lightly whisk the egg yolks, then whisk them into the honey mixture, then stir this into the walnuts and sugar. Pour the mixture into the pastry case and bake for 40 minutes until the tart is well caramelized. Leave to cool, then cut into thin wedges and serve with some crème fraîche.

Lavender fields of Provence

In Harold McGee's new book, the revised On Food and Cooking, *he dismisses a couple of the myths about making soufflés. First, it doesn't matter what you put on the inside of the dishes, be it butter, sugar or anything else, the mixture will inevitably rise. The other myth is that if you open the oven door while soufflés are cooking, they will collapse. Yes, they will, but as soon as you shut the oven door they will rise again. He goes on to explain that 'a hot oven and a thin mix will make a more dramatic rise than a thick mix, and a more dramatic collapse at the table'. This is quite a thin mix and creates a rise worthy of applause, but get to the table quick.*

Hot vanilla soufflés
with mango, passion fruit and lime sauce *Serves 4*

1 vanilla pod
300 ml full-cream milk
40 g butter, plus extra for greasing
25 g plain flour
4 large eggs, separated, plus 1 egg
  white

1 teaspoon vanilla extract
75 g caster sugar
Icing sugar, for dusting

FOR THE SAUCE:
4 ripe and wrinkly passion fruit
1 small, ripe, juicy mango, weighing
  about 450 g
2 tablespoons lime juice
1 tablespoon icing sugar, or to taste

Slit the vanilla pod open and scrape out the seeds. Put the milk, vanilla pod and seeds into a small pan, bring up to the boil then set aside for 30 minutes. Meanwhile, for the sauce, cut the passion fruit in half and scoop out the pulp into a sieve set over a bowl. Rub the juice through the sieve and discard the seeds. Peel the mango and slice the flesh away from the stone into a food processor. Blend until smooth, then press the purée through a sieve and stir in the passion fruit, lime juice and icing sugar. Pour into a serving jug, cover and chill.

Put a flat baking tray into the oven and preheat it to 190°C/Gas Mark 5. Lightly butter 4 individual soufflé dishes of 10 cm diameter and 6.5 cm deep (capacity about 375 ml).

Melt the butter in another small pan, stir in the flour and cook gently for 1 minute, stirring. Bring the milk back to the boil and then slowly strain onto the flour mixture, stirring all the time. Bring to the boil, still stirring, and leave to cook over a low heat for 2 minutes. Take the pan off the heat and beat in the egg yolks, one at a time, and the vanilla extract. Transfer the mixture to a large bowl.

Put the egg whites into another large, clean bowl and whisk until frothy, then gradually whisk in the sugar, a tablespoon at a time, into a soft, but not too stiff, glossy meringue. Gently fold into the vanilla custard, then divide the mixture between the prepared dishes. Smooth the tops with a palette knife. Place the dishes on the hot baking sheet and bake for 11 minutes. The soufflés should still be creamy in the centre.

Quickly transfer the soufflés to dessert plates, dust with icing sugar and take to the table. You make a small slit in the top of the soufflé and pour in the sauce.

Debbie came up with this one night while we were filming near Agen. We were standing underneath a fig tree, heavy with ripe figs that were rapidly being eaten by the birds and wasps. I said, 'They are so good – what can we do with them that's very simple?' And this is it. Sadly, fromage blanc hasn't made it over the Channel yet. It will, but in the meantime use a full-fat fromage frais instead.

Fresh figs with vanilla fromage blanc

Serves 6

12–18 ripe fresh figs	**1 vanilla pod**
400 g fromage blanc or fromage frais	**30 g caster sugar**

Trim the stalks from the figs, slice them in half and divide them between 6 dessert plates. Put the fromage blanc or fromage frais into a bowl. Slit the vanilla pod open length-ways, scrape out the seeds with the tip of a small knife and add them to the bowl along with the sugar. Mix together well, spoon onto the figs and serve.

Caramel mousse with almond brittle and strawberries *Serves 8*

FOR THE MOUSSE:
175 g granulated sugar
Juice 1 lemon (3 tablespoons)
1 x 11.5-g sachet powdered
   gelatine
3 medium eggs

2 medium egg yolks
50 g caster sugar
225 ml double cream

450 g small strawberries, halved, and
   crème fraîche, to serve

FOR THE ALMOND BRITTLE:
50 g blanched almonds
Vegetable oil, for greasing
150 g granulated sugar

For the mousse, put the granulated sugar and 150 ml cold water into a large, heavy-based pan. Leave over a low heat, stirring now and then, until the sugar has completely dissolved, then increase the heat and boil rapidly until the syrup has turned into a deep, amber-coloured caramel. Plunge the base of the pan into a sink of ice-cold water and leave to cool.

Add 5 tablespoons cold water to the now brittle caramel and warm through over a low heat until liquid once more. Set aside. Put the lemon juice into a small pan, sprinkle over the gelatine and set aside. Put the eggs, egg yolks and caster sugar into a large mixing bowl and whisk for about 8 minutes until the mixture is very thick and moussey and leaves a trail over the surface. Gradually whisk in the caramel syrup.

Warm the gelatine over a low heat until clear. Whip the cream into soft peaks. Gradually whisk the gelatine into the mousse, then rest the base of the bowl in lightly iced water and fold over until it shows signs of thickening. Gently fold in the cream, pour into a glass bowl and cover and chill until set.

For the almond brittle, preheat the oven to 190°C/Gas Mark 5. Spread the almonds on a baking sheet and roast for 9–10 minutes until a pale golden brown. Remove and leave to cool, then coarsely chop. Lightly oil a non-stick baking sheet and set to one side. Put the sugar and 150 ml cold water into a small pan and once again leave over a low heat until completely dissolved. Boil to an amber-coloured caramel, then quickly throw in the chopped nuts, swirl them around until well-coated, then pour onto the prepared baking sheet and tilt it back and forth until it has spread out into a thin even layer. Set aside and leave to set.

To serve, scoop spoonfuls of the mousse onto dessert plates. Break the caramel into large shards and rest alongside the mousse. Add a quenelle (spoonful) of crème fraîche and a pile of strawberries and serve.

This chocolate chestnut cake is sublimely subtle. It has a soft, melting, crumbly texture and the combination of good chocolate and chestnuts will make it seem like the most sophisticated gateau you ever ate, with a fluff of whipped cream and an espresso.

Gateau lyonnais
Rich chocolate and chestnut cake *Serves 8–10*

125 g unsalted butter, softened, plus
  extra for greasing
250 g chocolate, with at least 60%
  cocoa solids
1 x 435-g can unsweetened chestnut
  purée

1 teaspoon vanilla extract
1 tablespoon whisky or dark rum
6 large eggs, separated
Pinch of salt
175 g caster sugar
A little icing sugar, for dusting

Some cream or ice cream and an
  espresso, to serve

Preheat the oven to 180°C/Gas Mark 4. Lightly butter a 22-cm clip-sided tin and base line with non-stick baking parchment.

Break the chocolate into a bowl and rest over a pan of just-simmering water until melted. Remove the bowl from the pan and set to one side. Put the chestnut purée and butter into another bowl and beat together until smooth, then beat in the vanilla extract, whisky, egg yolks and melted chocolate.

In another large bowl, whisk the egg whites and salt until frothy, then gradually whisk in the caster sugar to form a very soft, glossy meringue-like mixture, but don't go on for too long as you don't want the mixture to get too stiff. Gently mix one-third into the chestnut and chocolate mixture to loosen it slightly, then fold in the remainder.

Pour the mixture into the prepared tin and bake for 45 minutes, until the cake has risen and is firm on top. It will look dry and cracked, but don't worry, this is how it should be. Remove and leave to cool in the tin for 20 minutes, then carefully remove from the tin, peel off the paper and transfer to a flat serving plate. Dust with icing sugar and serve warm or at room temperature with the cream or ice cream and an espresso.

The basis of this recipe came from Michel Guérard's restaurant at Eugénie-les-Bains near Pau in south-west France. The only alteration was to grill the peaches rather than poach them. The recipe is also extremely good made with fresh basil ice cream, but if you can get lemon verbena, it has just the right touch of delicate, lemony flavour. You could also try lemongrass as well. I haven't, but I bet it would be quite special.

Grilled peaches with lemon verbena ice cream and raspberries *Serves 6*

6 small, ripe and juicy peaches

4 tablespoons caster sugar, mixed
  with a few vanilla seeds if you wish

175 g raspberries

A few small lemon verbena leaves,
  to decorate (optional)

FOR THE LEMON VERBENA ICE CREAM:

300 ml full-cream milk

300 ml double cream

5 g lemon verbena leaves

5 large egg yolks

120 g caster sugar

2 teaspoons lemon juice

For the ice cream, put the milk, cream and lemon verbena leaves into a non-stick pan and bring slowly to the boil. Set aside for 30 minutes to allow the flavour of lemon verbena to infuse the milk.

Beat the egg yolks and sugar together in a bowl until creamy. Bring the milk back to the boil and strain onto the egg yolk mixture. Mix together well, return to the pan and cook over a gentle heat, stirring all the time, until the mixture is thick enough to coat the back of a wooden spoon. But don't let the custard boil or it will curdle. Leave to cool, then stir in the lemon juice and churn in an ice-cream maker until smooth. Transfer to a plastic container, cover and freeze for at least 3 hours or until needed.

To serve, preheat your grill to its highest setting. Halve the peaches, discarding the stones, and put them, cut-face up, in a shallow ovenproof dish. Sprinkle 1 teaspoon of sugar over each peach half and grill for 3 minutes or until the peaches have heated through and the sugar has started to caramelize.

Divide the peaches between 6 dessert plates and serve with a scoop of the lemon verbena ice cream and a small pile of raspberries. Decorate with small lemon verbena leaves if you wish.

Cherry pithiviers

Serves 8–10

2 x 350-g packets ready-rolled puff pastry, and butter for greasing

***Vanilla ice cream* (see page 207) or pouring cream, to serve**

FOR THE ALMOND PASTE FILLING:
125 g butter, softened
125 g caster sugar
1 medium egg
2 medium egg yolks

125 g ground almonds
15 g plain flour
2 tablespoons kirsch
225 g fresh cherries, stones removed
1 teaspoon icing sugar, for glazing

Ile d'Oléron

Unroll each sheet of puff pastry and cut a 25-cm disc from one piece and a 29-cm disc from the other, rolling them out a little more if necessary. Rest them in the fridge for 20 minutes.

For the almond paste filling, cream the butter and sugar together in a bowl until pale and fluffy. Beat in the egg and one of the egg yolks, then gently stir in the ground almonds, flour and kirsch. Stir in the pitted cherries.

Place the smaller disc of pastry onto a buttered baking sheet and mound the cherry and almond mixture into the centre, taking it to within 2.5 cm of the edge. Beat the remaining egg yolk with 1 teaspoon of cold water and brush a little around the edge of the pastry. Lay the second disc over the top of the filling and press the edges together to seal, pressing out any trapped air as you do so. Crimp the edges between your thumb and forefinger to give the edge an attractive finish, then chill the pudding for 20 minutes.

Meanwhile, preheat the oven to 220°C/Gas Mark 7. Brush the top of the pithiviers with the rest of the egg yolk glaze, then with the tip of a small, sharp knife, score radiating arcs from the centre out towards the edge, just into the surface of the pastry, taking care not to cut too deeply. Make a small hole in the centre to let the steam escape, and bake for 15–20 minutes until puffed up and richly golden. Lower the oven temperature to 180°C/Gas Mark 4 and continue to bake for 40 minutes or until a skewer pushed into the centre comes away clean. If it starts to get too brown, lay a sheet of foil loosely over the top.

To give the pithiviers its classic glazed appearance, remove it from the oven and increase the temperature once more to 220°C/Gas Mark 7. Dust the pastry with the icing sugar and return to the oven for 3–4 minutes until the sugar has caramelized and the tart has taken on a high gloss. Transfer to a cooling rack and leave to cool slightly, then serve warm, cut into wedges, with vanilla ice cream or pouring cream.

187

I'm a great fan of puff pastry tarts that consist of little more than a thin sheet of it, baked with sliced fruit on top and finished with a raspberry or apricot jam glaze. Particularly at dinner parties, it seems to me the perfect finish, because you can make them up beforehand and bung them in the oven while you're eating the main course. They always come out hot and crisp, and I love the way a dollop of crème fraîche melts on top. This one is just a little more complicated than those, as with the glaze I'm trying to create the flavour of pears poached in red wine. It uses half a bottle of Cabernet Sauvignon, reduced down with a little sugar to almost nothing, then warmed together with some redcurrant jelly to produce a deep-red glaze curiously reminiscent of mulled red wine, even though there are no spices in it.

Pear puff pastry tart with a red wine and redcurrant glaze *Serves 8*

¹/₂ x 75-cl bottle of gutsy, not too
  tannic red wine, such as an
  Australian Cabernet Sauvignon
25 g caster sugar, plus 2 teaspoons
75 g redcurrant jelly

500 g puff pastry
A little butter for greasing
4 firm dessert pears, such as
  Williams
Crème fraîche, to serve

Put the red wine in a small pan with the 2 teaspoons of sugar and boil rapidly until it has reduced to 2 tablespoons. Add the redcurrant jelly and stir until it has melted. Set aside.

Roll out the pastry on a lightly floured surface into a rectangle of approximately 28 x 38 cm. Lift onto a lightly greased baking sheet and prick the pastry here and there with a fork, leaving a 2.5-cm border clear around the edge. Chill for at least 20 minutes.

Preheat the oven to 200°C/Gas Mark 6. Peel, core and thinly slice the pears and arrange them, slightly overlapping, over the pastry, still leaving the border clear around the edge. Sprinkle with the remaining sugar and bake in the oven for 35–40 minutes until the pastry is crisp and golden and the pears are lightly browned.

Remove the tart from the oven. Warm through the glaze and brush generously over the pears. Cut the tart into rectangular pieces and serve warm with the crème fraîche.

*Gilles Pons's wine cellar in
Casseneuil, Lot-et-Garonne*

These are, as the title pretty much suggests, little pots of silky-smooth chocolate. In other words, there is no aeration, as with a mousse, just a few other ingredients to help the chocolate set softly. They are very rich so you only need to serve small portions.

Petit pots au chocolat
Little pots of chocolate *Makes 6*

225 g plain chocolate, with at least
  60% cocoa solids
15 g soft butter
4 egg yolks
150 ml double cream

150 ml full-cream milk
50 g caster sugar
6 teaspoons crème fraîche and a little
  cocoa powder, to decorate

Break the chocolate into a heatproof bowl and rest over a pan of just-simmering water. Leave until melted, then remove and stir until smooth. Stir in the softened butter and the egg yolks.

Put the cream, milk and sugar into a small pan, bring up to the boil and then stir into the chocolate mixture.

Pour the mixture into six 100-ml small tall pots, ramekins, small coffee cups or glass tumblers and leave somewhere cold to set, but do not refrigerate.

To serve, decorate the top of each pot with a tiny quenelle of crème fraîche and dust with a little cocoa powder.

L'épicerie flottante, the floating shop on the Canal du Midi at Le Somail

Normandy cider and apple sorbet
with crisp apple wafers *Serves 6–8*

Juice 1 lemon
300 ml Normandy apple cider
200 g caster sugar
75 g liquid glucose
2 kg Granny Smith apples

FOR THE CRISP APPLE WAFERS:
120 g caster sugar
2 teaspoons lemon juice
1 Granny Smith apple

Put the lemon juice, cider, sugar and liquid glucose into a pan and bring slowly to the boil, stirring occasionally until the sugar has dissolved. Remove from the heat and leave to cool.

Quarter, core and slice the unpeeled apples and pass through a juice extractor, working quickly before the juice can go brown; the yield should be about 1 litre. Skim off the layer of foam from the top and mix the juice with the cider syrup. Churn in an ice-cream maker until smooth, transfer to a plastic container, cover and freeze until firm: about 4 hours.

For the crisp apple wafers, preheat the oven to 90–100°C. Line a large, flat baking sheet with non-stick baking paper. Put the sugar and lemon juice into a pan with 120 ml water and bring to the boil, stirring. Pass through a fine sieve into a clean pan and keep hot. Slice the whole apple across very thinly by hand or with a mandolin. Pass the slices one at time through the syrup and place in a single layer on the tray. Put into the oven and leave to dry out for 2–3 hours until crisp. Remove, leave to cool, then keep in an airtight tin.

Remove the sorbet from the freezer a few minutes before serving to soften slightly. Serve scoops of the sorbet in tall glasses, each one garnished with apple wafers.

The idea for this recipe comes from a very good chef friend of mine, Luke Mangan. It's so successful because the spices are very subtle – it tastes like the best crème caramel you've ever had.

Crème caramel with cinnamon, cardamom and vanilla *Serves 6*

FOR THE CARAMEL:
175 g caster sugar
180 ml water

FOR THE CUSTARD:
500 ml full-cream milk
1 x 7.5-cm cinnamon stick
¹/₂ vanilla pod, split open lengthways

1 green cardamom pod, cracked open
100 g caster sugar
3 large eggs, plus 2 yolks

For the custard, put the milk, cinnamon stick, vanilla pod, cardamom pod and sugar into a pan and bring to the boil. Remove from the heat and leave for 1 hour for the flavours to infuse the milk.

Preheat the oven to 160°C/Gas Mark 3. Put a 1.5-litre shallow oval baking dish, measuring about 24 x 16 cm across the base, into the oven to warm. This will prevent it from cracking when you pour in the boiling hot caramel.

For the caramel, put the sugar and water into a heavy-based pan and leave over a very low heat, stirring now and then, until the sugar has dissolved. Then bring the syrup to the boil and leave to boil rapidly, without stirring, until it turns amber in colour. Remove from the heat and quickly pour into the warm baking dish. Set aside to cool.

Put the whole eggs and egg yolks into a bowl and whisk to combine. Whisk in the milk mixture, then strain into the baking dish (the mixture should be about 2.5 cm deep) and put the dish into a small roasting tin. Pour enough hot water into the tin to come halfway up the sides of the dish and bake in the oven for 45–50 minutes, until just set but still wobbly in the centre. It will continue to firm up after it comes out of the oven.

Remove the dish from the tray of water and leave to cool, then refrigerate overnight. To serve, carefully run a round-bladed knife around the edge of the dish, shake gently to make sure it is freed all round the edge, and quickly invert onto a flat oval serving dish.

These are a delight, and easy to make. The secret of success is the initial cooking of the butter, apples and soft brown sugar before transferring them to the moulds, topping with the almond sponge mixture and baking. This is just perfect for crème anglaise – custard, in other words. I'm sure my director, David Pritchard, would prefer Bird's, but not francophile me.

Baked apple and almond puddings
with crème anglaise *Serves 6*

FOR THE APPLES:
500 g dessert apples (about 4), such as Cox's or Braeburn
150 g unsalted butter
150 g light soft brown sugar

FOR THE ALMOND SPONGE:
175 g unsalted butter, softened
175 g caster sugar
3 medium eggs
100 g plain flour
100 g ground almonds
2 teaspoons baking powder

FOR THE CRÈME ANGLAISE:
1 vanilla pod
600 ml full cream milk
5 egg yolks
3 tablespoons caster sugar

For the crème anglaise, slit open the vanilla pod and scrape out the seeds with the tip of a sharp knife. Put the milk, vanilla pod and seeds into a non-stick pan and bring to the boil. Remove the pan from the heat and set aside for 20 minutes or so to allow the flavour of vanilla to infuse the milk. Cream the egg yolks and sugar together in a bowl until smooth. Bring the milk back to the boil, remove the vanilla pod and gradually beat the milk into the egg yolks and sugar. Return the mixture to the pan, and cook over a medium heat, stirring constantly, until the custard thickens, but don't let it boil. Set aside and keep warm.

Preheat the oven to 180°C/Gas Mark 4. Peel, core and thickly slice the apples. Put the butter and sugar into a medium-sized pan and melt over a low heat, add the apples and cook for 5 minutes until just tender. Lift the apples out of the buttery juices with a slotted spoon and drop into the base of six 250-ml mini pudding basins or ramekins. Spoon 1 teaspoon of the buttery mixture over the top of the apples and reserve the remainder.

For the almond sponge, cream the butter and sugar together in a bowl until pale and creamy. Beat in the eggs one at a time, adding a little flour with the last egg to stop the mixture curdling. Sift over the rest of the flour with the baking powder, and fold in with the ground almonds. Divide the mixture between the dishes and lightly level the surface. Bake for 35–40 minutes, covering them with a loose sheet of foil after about 30 minutes if they are browning too quickly, until a skewer, pushed into the centre of one of the puddings, comes away clean.

Shortly before the puddings are ready, bring the reserved butter and sugar mixture to the boil and boil rapidly for about 2 minutes until reduced to a rich toffee sauce.

To serve, run a round-bladed knife around the edge of the puddings and invert onto warmed plates. Spoon some of the toffee sauce over and around the puddings and serve with the crème anglaise.

Passion fruit crème brûlée
with passion fruit jellies *Makes 8–10*

300 ml full-cream milk
700 ml double cream
¹/₂ vanilla pod (cut across the centre)
12 ripe and wrinkly passion fruit
10 large egg yolks

150 g caster sugar
Icing sugar, for dusting

FOR THE PASSION FRUIT JELLIES:
8–10 ripe and wrinkly passion fruit
75 g caster sugar
125 ml water
1¹/₂ x 5-g leaves of gelatine

For the crème brûlées, put the milk, cream and vanilla pod into a pan and bring to just below boiling point. Set aside for 1 hour, to allow time for the flavour of vanilla to infuse the milk and cream.

Meanwhile, cut the passion fruit in half and scrape out the pulp into a sieve set over a bowl. Rub the pulp through with a wooden spoon – you want about 150 ml of juice.

Preheat the oven to 120°C/Gas Mark ¹/₂. Mix the egg yolks and sugar together in a bowl, then strain onto the cream and milk mixture and stir in the passion fruit juice. Pour the mixture into 8–10 x 175-ml ramekins and put them into a roasting tin. Pour hot, but not boiling, water into the tin so that it comes halfway up the sides of the ramekins. Bake for approximately 1 hour until just set but still slightly wobbly in the centre.

Remove the dishes from the hot water and leave to cool, then cover and chill overnight.

For the passion fruit jellies, pulp and sieve the passion fruit as before, reserving 2 table-spoons of the seeds. Peel away the thin membrane lining the passion fruit half-shells and then put the shells into empty egg boxes, ready to fill with the jelly.

Put the passion fruit juice, sugar and water into a small pan and warm through over a gentle heat to dissolve the sugar, but don't let it get too hot. Meanwhile, soak the leaf gelatine in a bowl of tepid water until soft, then lift out, drop into the jelly mixture and stir until dissolved. Pour 5 tablespoons of the jelly mixture into a small bowl and set aside.

Fill the passion fruit shells almost to the top with the jelly mixture and chill in the fridge until set. Meanwhile, wash off the reserved passion fruit seeds and stir them into the reserved jelly mixture. When the first lot of jelly has set, spoon some of the seeded jelly mixture in a thin layer over the top of each one and return to the fridge to set.

Shortly before serving, dust the top of each crème brûlée with 1 teaspoon of icing sugar and, holding a blow torch about 10–12 cm away from the surface, caramelize the sugar evenly. Leave for a few minutes to harden, then transfer to dessert plates and place 2 of the jellies alongside each one. Serve straight away.

This is the sort of dessert that will keep in the freezer, well covered, for a couple of weeks, but no longer I suggest. One of the things that impresses me about lunch and dinner in France is how little is actually cooked there and then. Of course, having the back-up of fantastic food shops, such as traiteurs, charcuteries and patisseries, does make all the difference. The result is that four-course meals are easy to put together, and I honestly think this is why the French don't get fat. Four small courses is so much better for you than one large main course. Tuck these little parfaits in your freezer for use the following week, then defrost for 20–30 minutes to soften slightly before serving. They are much nicer served slightly icy in the centre.

Raspberry and vanilla parfait *Makes 8*

100 g caster sugar
3 tablespoons water
6 medium egg yolks

350 g raspberries
2 vanilla pods
300 ml double cream

100 g extra raspberries and a little
icing sugar, to decorate

Put the sugar and water into a small saucepan and leave over a low heat until clear. Bring to the boil and boil rapidly for 2 minutes. At the same time, put the egg yolks into a bowl and whisk with a hand-held electric mixer for 3 minutes until pale and slightly moussey. Then slowly add the syrup to the yolks, whisking all the time, and continue to whisk for 5 minutes until the mixture is very thick and about 3 times its original volume.

Put the raspberries into a bowl and crush them with the back of a fork into a coarse purée. Slit open the vanilla pods and scrape the seeds into another bowl. Add the cream and whisk until it forms soft peaks, then gently fold into the egg mixture, followed by the crushed raspberries.

Divide the mixture between 8 x 180-ml small, deep dishes or ramekins, cover well with clingfilm and freeze for at least 4 hours.

To serve, remove the parfaits from the freezer and leave to soften slightly at room temperature. Pile a few raspberries into the centre, dust with a little icing sugar and serve.

This is the recipe of a pastry chef at the Seafood Restaurant, who changed our dessert menu from treacle tart and bread and butter pudding into what it is today. David Pope, who now makes his own fantastic chocolates and cakes – David's Patisserie at Wadebridge – was also a great teacher to other chefs. I wish I could get him to work for us at the cookery school. This tart is one of his best and still on the menu.

Redcurrant tart *Serves 10–12*

FOR THE PASTRY:
The ingredients for 1 quantity *Sweet pastry* (see page 211), and extra butter for greasing
Finely grated zest of ¹/₂ orange
Finely grated zest of ¹/₂ lemon

FOR THE FILLING:
4 medium eggs, beaten
375 g fresh redcurrants, stalks removed
1 vanilla pod
160 g icing sugar, sifted

2 tablespoons plain flour
300 ml double cream

Crème fraîche, to serve

For the pastry case, sift the flour, salt and icing sugar into a food processor or bowl, add the pieces of chilled butter and the orange and lemon zest and work together briefly, either in the food processor or with your fingertips, until the mixture looks like fine breadcrumbs. Stir in the egg yolk, mixed with enough water so that the mixture starts to come together into a ball, then turn out on to a lightly floured surface and knead very briefly until smooth.

Roll out the pastry on a lightly floured surface and use to line a greased loose-bottomed flan tin that is 4 cm deep and 23 cm across the base. Prick the base here and there with a fork and chill for 20–30 minutes.

Preheat the oven to 200°C/Gas Mark 6. Line the pastry case with crumpled grease-proof paper, cover the base with a thin layer of baking beans and bake for 12–15 minutes until the edges are biscuit-coloured. Carefully remove the paper and baking beans and return the pastry case to the oven for 3–4 minutes. Remove, brush the base with a little of the beaten egg and return to the oven once more for 2 minutes. Remove and lower the oven temperature to 150°C/Gas Mark 2.

Scatter the redcurrants over the base of the pastry case. Slit open the vanilla pod and scrape out the seeds with the tip of a small knife (save the vanilla pod for later use or drop it into a jar of caster sugar). Mix the eggs with the vanilla seeds, icing sugar and flour until smooth, then add the cream and mix together. Strain the mixture over the redcurrants and bake for approximately 1 hour or until just set.

Remove and leave to cool slightly, then remove from the tin and serve warm, cut into wedges with some crème fraîche.

I have to confess that this recipe came out of an enthusiasm for Marcel Proust's A la Recherche du Temps Perdu. *Since the memory of madeleines served with a lime tea was the catalyst for his charming memories of childhood, I had to fit it in somewhere. And as it happened, we had just been filming Denis Cournol and his bees, and the addition of a little honey to a madeleine is delightful. Combine that with some apricots poached with vanilla and a little more honey, served together with vanilla ice cream, and you have the sort of dessert that the French are justly famous for.*

Vanilla poached apricots with honey madeleines

Serves 6

FOR THE VANILLA AND HONEY POACHED APRICOTS:
1 kg fresh apricots
2 vanilla pods
150 g clear honey
500 ml water
Juice of 1 lemon, strained

FOR THE MADELEINES:
3 medium eggs
100 g caster sugar
Finely grated zest of 1 lemon
100 g plain flour, sifted, plus extra for dusting
1 teaspoon baking powder

100 g butter, melted, plus extra for greasing the tins
1 tablespoon clear honey

Vanilla ice cream (see page 207), to serve (optional)

For the apricots, halve the fruit and remove the stones. Spilt the vanilla pods in half length-ways and scrape out the seeds with the tip of a small, sharp knife. Put the honey, vanilla pods, seeds and water into a medium-sized pan and leave over a low heat until the honey has dissolved. Add the apricots and simmer gently for 5–10 minutes, depending on the ripeness of your fruit, until just tender. Lift the apricots and vanilla pod out with a slotted spoon into a serving bowl, return the pan of syrup to a high heat and boil rapidly until reduced by half. Add the lemon juice and leave to cool, then strain back over the apricots, cover and set aside until needed.

For the madeleines, brush 2 x 12-cake madeleine moulds with melted butter and set aside for a few minutes until the butter has set. Then dust with flour, tapping out the excess. This will ensure that only the smallest amount of flour sticks to the butter, giving the madeleines a better finish. Preheat the oven to 190°C/Gas Mark 5.

Put the eggs and sugar into a large bowl and whisk with a hand-held electric mixer for 3 minutes until thick and moussey. Whisk in the lemon zest. Sift the plain flour and baking powder together and gently fold in, followed by the melted butter and the honey. Place the batter in the fridge and leave for 15 minutes to thicken slightly.

Fill each of the moulds three-quarters full with the mixture and bake for 10 minutes until puffed up and golden. Leave to cool, then carefully remove from the tins.

To serve, put 2 madeleines to one side of each of 6 shallow dessert bowls. Spoon some of the apricots and a little syrup alongside. Add a scoop or two of ice cream if you wish. Store the rest of the madeleines in an airtight tin and eat within a couple of days.

Accompaniments

Pommes vapeur

Steamed potatoes

Choose 1 kg uniform sized slightly waxy potatoes, each weighing between 100 and 150 g and measuring about 7 cm in length. You can use potatoes such as Charlotte, Ratte (also known as Cornichon or Asparges), Belle de Fontenay, Pink Fir Apple, Jersey Royals or red-skinned Roseval. Using a small sharp kitchen knife, peel the potatoes from top to bottom, taking as wide a band of peel off each time as possible, and work around the potato to create a fairly uniform oval shape. Bring 2 cm water to the boil in a large pan, then reduce to a simmer. Lower a petal steamer into the pan (the boiling water should not reach the holes), add the potatoes and sprinkle them liberally with salt. Cover with a tight-fitting lid and steam for about 20 minutes, checking the water level regularly, until tender when pierced with the tip of a small knife, but not falling apart. Remove the potatoes from the pan, brush them with a little melted butter and sprinkle, if you wish, with some chopped parsley.
Serves 4.

Pommes purée

Puréed potatoes

Cut 1 kg peeled floury potatoes such as Maris Piper or King Edwards into 5-cm chunks and put into a pan of well-salted water (1 teaspoon per 600 ml), bring to the boil and simmer for 20 minutes or until tender. Drain and leave until the steam has died down – this will ensure that they are perfectly dry. Press through a potato ricer or mouli légumes – to make a perfectly smooth purée a hand masher is not suitable – back into the pan and add 150 ml full-cream milk or cream and 50 g butter, and beat vigorously over a low heat until light and very smooth. Season to taste. *Serves 4.*

Celeriac and potato mash

Cut 450 g peeled floury potatoes and 450 g peeled celeriac into chunks. Put them into separate pans of well-salted water (1 teaspoon per 600 ml) and add 2 lemon slices to the pan of celeriac to stop it from discolouring. Bring to the boil and cook for 20 minutes until tender. Drain both well, discarding the lemon slices from the celeriac, and pass them both through a potato ricer back into one pan. Stir in 50 g butter, 1 crushed garlic clove and some salt and pepper to taste. *Serves 4.*

Pommes frites and other chips

Peel 550 g medium-sized floury potatoes, such as Maris Piper or King Edwards. For pommes frites (i.e. thin chips), cut the potatoes into slices 5 mm thick and then lengthways into thin chips; for roughly cut chips cut the potatoes into wedges; and for goose-fat chips (see below), cut them into slices 1 cm thick and then lengthways into chips 2 cm wide. Quickly rinse under cold water to remove the starch and then dry them well on a clean tea towel. Next, the oil. I like to cook most chips in groundnut oil, as it is more stable at higher temperatures, but sunflower and vegetable oil are fine, too. They are also fantastic cooked in olive oil for certain dishes – just ordinary olive oil, not extra virgin. For goose-fat chips, you will need to empty about two 340-g cans of goose fat into a medium-sized pan so that when it has melted you have a sufficient depth in which to cook the chips – the pan should not be more than one-third full. Heat the oil or goose fat to 120°C. Drop a large handful of the chips into a chip basket, lower it into the oil and cook them in batches for about 5 minutes until they are tender when pierced with the tip of a knife, but have not taken on any colour. Lift them out and leave to drain, then chill if you don't want to cook them straight away. To finish, heat the oil or fat to 190°C and cook in batches for about 2 minutes until crisp and golden. Drain on kitchen paper, then sprinkle with salt and serve straight away. *Serves 4.*

Sautéed potatoes

Cut 750 g peeled floury potatoes into 4 cm pieces. Put them into a pan of well-salted water (1 teaspoon per 600 ml), bring to the boil and simmer until tender – about 7 minutes. Drain well and leave until the steam has died down. Heat 40 g butter and 3 tablespoons olive oil in a large, heavy-based frying pan. It's important not to overcrowd the pan, so if you have not got a really large pan, use 2 smaller ones. Add the potatoes and fry them over a medium heat for about 10 minutes, turning them over as they brown, until they are crisp, golden brown and sandy – the outside of the potatoes should break off a little as you sauté them, giving them a nice crumbly, crunchy crust. Season with a little salt and freshly ground black pepper and serve straight away. *Serves 4.*

Roast potatoes

Preheat the oven to 220°C/Gas Mark 7. Cut 1 kg peeled floury potatoes into 5-cm chunks. Put into a pan of well-salted water (1 teaspoon per 600 ml), bring to the boil and simmer for 10 minutes until soft on the outside, but still slightly hard in the centre. Drain and leave for the steam to die down, then return them to the pan, cover with a lid and shake gently to rough up the edges a little. Heat a thin layer of sunflower oil or goose fat in a large roasting tin, add the potatoes and turn them over once or twice until well coated. Drain off any surplus fat and roast them in the top of the oven, turning the potatoes over halfway through, for 1 hour until crisp and richly golden. *Serves 4.*

Pommes Anna

Preheat the oven to 220°C/Gas Mark 7. Peel 1.25 kg floury potatoes and slice them very thinly on a mandolin, by hand or using the slicing blade of a food processor. Heat a sloping-sided, heavy-based mould with a base measurement of 20 cm, such as a tarte tatin mould or ovenproof frying pan, on the top of the stove over a medium heat. Add 25 g butter and, when melted, take some trouble to get the first layer of potatoes neatly overlapped over the base as this is what you will see when it's turned out. Layer in the rest of the potatoes, seasoning each layer with some salt and pepper and top with another 25 g butter pieces. Transfer the mould or frying pan to the oven and bake for 1 hour. To serve, invert on to a warm serving plate and cut into wedges. *Serves 6.*

Pommes Coq d'Or

Preheat the oven to 180°C/Gas Mark 4. Boil 900 ml *Chicken stock* (see page 208) until reduced to 175 ml and then

leave to cool slightly. Mash 2 garlic cloves with a little salt under the blade of a knife into a smooth paste and stir into the stock with 1 teaspoon salt and 20 turns of the black pepper mill. Peel 750 g floury potatoes and slice them very thinly on a mandolin, by hand or using the slicing blade of a food processor. Liberally butter the inside of a large cast-iron gratin dish. Layer the potatoes in the dish, overlapping the slices slightly as you go, starting on the outside and working inwards. The potatoes should be a maximum of three layers thick. Add the chicken stock, which should come just below the top layer of potatoes, and dot the top with 25 g butter. Cook for 1 hour. *Serves 4.*

Saffron potatoes

Put 900 ml cold *Chicken stock* (see page 208) and 1 kg of peeled evenly sized potatoes (those measuring about 5 cm) into a pan. Bring to the boil, add a pinch of saffron strands along with ½ teaspoon salt and simmer for 15–20 minutes until tender. Drain and serve straight away. *Serves 4.*

Boulangère potatoes

This is not a traditional way of cooking a boulangère, where sliced potatoes and onions are slowly cooked from raw with stock. Par-cooking them first in a well-flavoured stock with some thyme and butter ensures a much more consistent and concentrated flavour to the finished dish and also halves the cooking time. Preheat the oven to 200°C/Gas Mark 6 and lightly butter a 1.5-litre shallow ovenproof dish. Peel 1 kg floury potatoes and cut them into slices about 5 mm thick; thinly slice 1 medium onion. Bring 350 ml *Chicken stock* (see page 208) to the boil in a pan, add 50 g butter, the leaves from 4 sprigs of thyme, the potatoes, onions, ½ teaspoon salt and some black pepper. Bring to a simmer and cook gently for about 5 minutes, until the potatoes are tender when pierced with a knife. Layer the potatoes and onions in the

dish, finishing the top layer neatly if you wish, and pour over any remaining stock. Bake for 40–45 minutes until the potatoes are lightly golden. *Serves 4.*

Pommes dauphinoise

Preheat the oven to 190°C/Gas Mark 5. Peel 900 g potatoes and slice them very thinly on a mandolin, by hand or using the slicing blade of a food processor, and put them into a bowl. Mix together 300 ml crème fraîche or double cream and 300 ml milk with some seasoning to taste, add to the potatoes and mix well. Lightly butter a 1.5-litre shallow ovenproof dish and rub with 1 crushed clove of garlic, then spoon in the potatoes, overlapping the top layer of potato slices neatly if you wish. Bake in the oven for 1¼ hours, or until the potatoes are cooked through and the top is golden and bubbling. *Serves 6.*

L'aligot
Cheese and potato purée

This dish would also make a nice light lunch served with French bread and a

salad. Peel 900 g floury potatoes, put them into a pan of cold, lightly salted water, bring to the boil and simmer for 20 minutes or until tender. Drain and leave until the steam has died down, then pass through a potato ricer or mouli légumes back into the pan. Heat 150 ml double cream and 50 g butter in a small pan, then stir into the potatoes, with 1 small crushed clove of garlic, over a gentle heat until the potatoes are smooth and hot. If the mixture seems a little stiff, add a little more cream. This will all depend on how dry and floury your potatoes were. Now stir in 275 g thinly sliced Tomme de Cantal cheese (or Tilsit cheese) and stir rapidly until the mixture is very smooth and forms ribbons as the wooden spoon is lifted. Take care not to let the mixture get too hot now or the cheese will overcook and harden and the mixture will go grainy. Swiftly remove the pan from the heat, season to taste and serve. *Serves 4.*

Roasted sweet potatoes with olive oil and herbes de Provence

This recipe also works well with carrots or prepared squash. Peel 750 g sweet potatoes and cut them into 7 cm chunks. Put 3 tablespoons olive oil, 2 sliced garlic cloves, 1 teaspoon dried herbes de Provence and 2 tablespoons dry white wine into a small roasting tin. Add the potatoes, 1 teaspoon sea salt flakes and some ground black pepper and toss together well. Roast at 220°C/Gas Mark 7 for 20–25 minutes until golden brown on the outside and soft in the centre. *Serves 4.*

Spätzle

Homemade flour and egg noodles

Sift 175 g plain flour into a bowl, make a well in the centre and add 3 medium eggs. Gradually beat the flour into the eggs, adding 50–85 ml milk bit by bit until you have a smooth, very thick batter. Bring a large pan of well-salted water to the boil (1 teaspoon per 600 ml). Press the batter through a potato ricer fitted with the disc with the largest holes, into the boiling water to create short, fat noodles. Cook for 1 minute then drain through a colander, transfer to a clean tea towel and leave to drain well. Melt 25 g butter in a large pan, add the spätzle and fry over a medium heat for 2 minutes, turning frequently, until hot and lightly golden. Add 1 tablespoon chopped parsley and some salt and pepper to taste, toss together briefly and serve. *Serves 4.*

Petit pois à la française

Remove the outer leaves from 4 little gem lettuce hearts if necessary, trim the bases and slice each one across quite finely. Trim 12 spring onions and cut into 2.5-cm pieces or peel 225 g tiny button onions. Melt 25 g butter in a shallow, flameproof casserole dish, add the onions and cook for 2–3 minutes until tender but not browned. Add 700 g fresh or frozen petit pois, the lettuce, 100 ml water, $\frac{1}{2}$ teaspoon sugar and some salt and freshly ground white pepper, and simmer rapidly for 3–4 minutes until the peas have started to soften and about $\frac{3}{4}$ of the liquid has evaporated. Now dot another 25 g butter around the pan and sprinkle over 1 tablespoon chopped chervil.

Shake the pan over the heat until the butter has melted and amalgamated with the cooking juices to make a sauce. *Serves 4.*

Haricots verts au beurre Gascon

Green beans with mild garlic butter

Drop 6 large unpeeled cloves of garlic into a small pan of boiling water and simmer over a low heat for 10–15 minutes or until very tender. Drain and, when cool enough to handle, peel and mash on a board with the blade of a large knife until smooth. Transfer the paste to a bowl and mix in 75 g soft, unsalted butter and some seasoning to taste. Drop 700 g prepared fine green beans into a pan of boiling salted water and cook for 4 minutes or until tender, then drain well and return to the pan. Add the garlic butter and toss together briefly. Check the seasoning and serve immediately. *Serves 4.*

Yellow beans with pistou

Put 3 large garlic cloves into a mini food processor and finely chop. Add 25 g basil leaves and 50 g finely grated Parmesan and blend until the basil is finely chopped. Then, with the machine still running, gradually add 4 tablespoons extra virgin olive oil to make a smooth paste. Transfer the mixture to a bowl and set aside. Drop the prepared beans into a pan of boiling salted water and cook for 4 minutes or until tender. Drain well, return to the pan with the pistou and toss together well. Check the seasoning and serve immediately. *This amount of pistou will be sufficient to coat 700–900 g prepared beans, enough to feed 4–6 people.*

Broad beans in garlic cream sauce

This is also a very good way of serving cooked fine green beans. Cook 600 g shelled broad beans in boiling salted water for 2–3 minutes until tender. Drain and, if young, leave as they are, but if slightly older, remove their tough outer skins if you wish. Soften 2 finely chopped garlic cloves in 2 tablespoons extra virgin olive oil in a wide, shallow pan. Add 2 tablespoons white wine vinegar and a large pinch of caster sugar and simmer until almost all the liquid has disappeared. Add 85 ml double cream, bring to the boil and simmer until the sauce has reduced and thickened. Add the cooked beans and simmer a few minutes longer until the sauce coats the beans. Add 1 teaspoon chopped thyme or summer savory and 1 tablespoon chopped parsley and season with salt to taste. *Serves 4.*

Haricots blancs with bacon and cream

Soak 225 g dried haricots beans overnight in plenty of water. The next day, drain, cover with 2.5 litres fresh water and bring to the boil, skimming off the scum as it rises to the surface. Reduce the heat, add a bouquet garni of thyme, bay leaves and parsley stalks and leave to simmer for 30 minutes to 1 hour until tender. Only add 1 teaspoon salt to the water 10 minutes before the end of cooking. Drain and set aside. Heat 2 tablespoons olive oil in a pan, add 4 diced rashers of thick-cut rindless smoked streaky bacon and fry until lightly golden. Add the cooked beans, 5 tablespoons double cream and simmer gently until the sauce has thickened, shaking the pan, rather than stirring, so as not to break up the beans. Add 2 tablespoons finely chopped parsley, season to taste and serve. *Serves 4.*

Vichy carrots

Trim and scrape 450 g young spring carrots. If they are small, leave them whole, otherwise slice them on the diagonal into 2 or 3 pieces each. Put into a heavy-based pan with 25 g butter, a pinch of salt, 2 lumps of sugar (about 1 teaspoon) and 450 ml water. The water of the Vichy region is slightly minerally; you could add a pinch of bicarbonate of soda to ordinary tap water to help achieve the same effect. Cook the carrots, uncovered, for 20–25 minutes until nearly all the water has evaporated and they are tender. Add another lump of butter and shake the pan to prevent the carrots from sticking and to cover them in a glossy glaze. Add a little chopped parsley, toss briefly and serve. *Serves 4.*

Carrots provençal

Heat 2 tablespoons extra virgin olive oil in a large, deep frying pan over a medium-high heat. Add 450 g trimmed and scrubbed baby carrots, toss until well coated in the oil, then cover, reduce the heat to medium and cook for 8–10 minutes, shaking the pan every now and then, until just tender. Uncover the pan, add $1/2$ a clove of finely chopped garlic and season with a little salt. Cook for a further minute, then add 1 tablespoon chopped parsley, toss together briefly and serve. *Serves 4.*

Melange of baby spring vegetables

Gently heat 50 ml extra virgin olive oil in a large sauté pan. Add 700 g of any combination of the following vegetables in order of how long they will take to cook: young carrots, prepared and sliced artichoke hearts, baby courgettes, shelled peas, mangetout, spinach, haricots verts, just-cooked baby new potatoes, trimmed and halved spring onions and a little finely chopped garlic. When the vegetables are cooked, stir in a small bunch of flat-leaf parsley sprigs, halved chive stalks and dill sprigs, and when the herbs have just wilted down, season with a little salt and pepper and serve. *Serves 4.*

Courgettes with tarragon and chives

If you can get hold of very small, just-picked courgettes all the better. Slice 700 g young courgettes across into thin discs. Melt 50 g butter in a large sauté pan. Add the courgettes and fry them gently over a low heat until just tender, sprinkling them with about 2 tablespoons each of chopped tarragon and chives and a little salt and freshly ground black pepper about 1 minute after they have started cooking. *Serves 4.*

Fennel and Parmesan gratin

This also works very well with prepared Swiss chard or halved heads of chicory. The chard stalks will take 10 minutes, the leaves 3 minutes and the chicory 4 minutes. Remove the outer layer from 1.25 kg (about 8 small) fennel bulbs and slice them lengthways through the root into 5-mm thick slices. Drop into a pan of well-salted boiling water (1 teaspoon per 600 ml) and cook for 8–10 minutes until just tender. Drain well, transfer to a bowl and toss with 125 ml crème fraîche and some salt and pepper to taste. Spoon into a large, well-buttered gratin dish, spread out into an even layer and sprinkle with 75 g finely grated Parmesan cheese. Preheat the grill to high, place the gratin dish about 12.5 cm away from the heat and grill for 5 minutes or until the cheese is golden and bubbling. *Serves 6.*

Steamed green cabbage

Remove the outer leaves from 1 medium-sized green cabbage, quarter, remove the core and cut each piece lengthways into slices 1 cm thick. Put 1 cm water into the base of a large pan, add 1 teaspoon salt and the cabbage and cook over a vigorous heat, turning over now and then, for 3–4 minutes or until just tender. Drain and serve immediately. *Serves 4.*

Sautéed white cabbage with bacon and juniper

Remove the outer leaves from a 750-g white cabbage, cut it into quarters, remove the core and shred finely. Drop into a large pan of boiling salted water and bring back to the boil for about 3 minutes then drain and refresh under cold water. Drain well. Cut 150 g rindless smoked streaky bacon across into thin strips. Heat 1 teaspoon olive oil in a large deep frying pan, add the bacon and fry until beginning to brown. Add 15 g butter, 6 crushed juniper berries, the cabbage and seasoning, stir well, cover and cook very gently for 5 minutes until just tender. *Serves 4.*

Roasted baby beetroot with mustard vinaigrette

Preheat the oven to 180°C/Gas Mark 4. If your beetroot still have their tops, cut them off, leaving about 2.5 cm of stalk on each root. Wash them fairly gently, especially if small and young, so that you remove any soil but don't break the skin. Toss them in a couple of tablespoons olive oil and some sea salt flakes, then lay them in a roasting tin and cover tightly with foil. Bake for 1–2 hours. Check them after 1 hour with a skewer and if you meet no resistance in the centre of the root, they are ready. Remove from the oven and leave to cool, still covered, for about 10 minutes, as this will help the skins to loosen. Meanwhile, make the mustard vinaigrette. Whisk 1 tablespoon Dijon mustard and 1 tablespoon white wine vinegar together in a small bowl. Gradually whisk in 5 tablespoons extra virgin olive oil to make a thick dressing. Season to taste with salt and pepper. Uncover the beetroot and peel by gently pushing off the skins with your fingers. The smaller the beetroot, the easier this is. If the beetroot are small, leave them whole, otherwise slice them and lay them over the base of a shallow dish. Spoon over the dressing, scatter over a little chopped parsley and toss together gently. Serve while still warm.
Serves 4.

Roasted pumpkin with chilli and garlic

This recipe works well with wedges of any type of squash, particularly butternut, kabocha and acorn. Preheat the oven to 200°C/Gas Mark 6. Cut 900 g–1.5 kg pumpkin or squash into wedges 2.5 cm wide and scoop out the seeds. Put 2 teaspoons coriander seeds and $1/2$ teaspoon fennel seeds into a mortar or a spice grinder and work into a coarse powder. Tip into a roasting tin and add 1 finely chopped garlic clove, $1/4$ teaspoon chilli flakes, 1 teaspoon sea salt flakes, 1 teaspoon coarsely crushed black pepper and 3 tablespoons olive oil. Mix together well, then add the wedges of squash and turn them over a few times in the olive oil mixture until they are well coated. Turn them all flesh-side up and roast in the oven for 20–30 minutes or until tender.
Serves 6.

Frisée salad with mustard dressing

Cut away the pale green leaves from the centre of 1 curly endive, close to the base, and separate into leaves. Wash well and dry in a salad spinner. Discard the remaining, dark green leaves, which are hard and very bitter. Whisk 1 teaspoon Dijon mustard and 1 teaspoon white wine vinegar together in a small bowl and then slowly whisk in 5 teaspoons sunflower oil to make a thick, emulsified dressing. Season to taste with salt and pepper. Toss this with the leaves just before serving.
Serves 4.

Green lettuce salad with Orléanais dressing

For the dressing, put 1 small garlic clove onto a board and lightly crush with the side of a knife. Sprinkle with a pinch of salt and mash with the blade of the knife until smooth. Put into a small bowl and add 2 tablespoons good red wine vinegar, such as Paul Corcelet or Maille, 1 teaspoon Dijon mustard and $1/2$ teaspoon sugar. Whisk together briefly then gradually whisk in 8 tablespoons olive oil and $1/4$ teaspoon salt. Break 2 green-leaf lettuce, such as escarole, soft round lettuce, butterhead, Batavia or 4–6 little gem lettuce into separate leaves, wash and dry well in a salad spinner. Break the leaves into a salad bowl and toss with 3 tablespoons of the dressing. *The dressing makes enough for 3 salads, but keeps well in the fridge. Serves 4.*

Radicchio and oakleaf salad with sherry vinegar dressing

For the dressing, mix 2 tablespoons sherry vinegar, 1 teaspoon Dijon mustard, 1 teaspoon clear honey, $1/4$ teaspoon salt and some freshly ground black pepper together in a bowl. Gradually whisk in 8 tablespoons vegetable oil and adjust the seasoning to taste. Discard any damaged outside leaves from 2 oakleaf lettuces, then break the remainder into smaller leaves. Break half a head of radicchio into smaller pieces, similar to those of the oakleaf, and wash both gently, drain and dry well in a salad spinner. Mix together in a bowl. Heat 2 teaspoons vegetable oil in a frying pan over a low heat, add 25 g pine nuts and sauté for about 2 minutes until golden. Remove with a slotted spoon and leave to drain on kitchen paper. Stir 1 tablespoon chopped parsley into the salad dressing, add about 3 tablespoons to the lettuce leaves, enough to lightly coat the leaves, then sprinkle with the pine nuts. *This dressing is enough for 2 salads. Serves 6.*

Patricia Wells's cheesemaker's salad

Put 2 thinly sliced shallots, separated into rings, and 1 tablespoon good red wine vinegar into a large, shallow salad bowl. Toss them together and set aside – for at least 15 minutes and anything up to 4 hours – to soften the shallots. When you are ready to serve, add the washed and dried leaves from 1 mild, delicately flavoured green lettuce, such as a butterhead or soft round lettuce, and toss to coat with the vinegar and shallots. Season with

some salt, add 2–3 tablespoons double cream and toss together very gently to coat all the leaves. Serve straight away. *Serves 4.*

Concombre à la crème
Cucumber salad with dill and cream

Peel 1 large cucumber and thinly slice, by hand or on a mandolin. Put 2 very thinly sliced shallots and 2 teaspoons white wine vinegar into a bowl and leave to soften for 20 minutes. After 10 minutes, toss the sliced cucumber with a large pinch of salt in a colander and leave to drain for 10 minutes. Add the cucumber to the bowl of shallots with 2 teaspoons chopped dill, 2 tablespoons double cream and some freshly ground white pepper to taste and mix together briefly. Serve straight away. *Serves 4.*

Tomato salad with spring onions and a lemon, herb and olive oil dressing

Thinly slice 6 medium-sized vine-ripened tomatoes and overlap them over the base of a shallow dish, discarding the top and bottom slices. Thinly slice the white part of 2 spring onions and scatter over the tomatoes. Finely chop the green part and set aside. For the dressing, put 2 tablespoons strained lemon juice into a small bowl with some salt and pepper and then whisk in 6 tablespoons extra virgin olive oil. Stir in the chopped green spring onion, 1 small crushed garlic clove, 1 tablespoon chopped parsley and 1 tablespoon chopped basil. Pour sufficient dressing over the tomatoes to moisten them, and serve. *Serves 4.*

Marinated bean and spring onion salad

Top and tail 600 g mixed green and yellow French beans and then break them in half. Drop into a pan of boiling salted water (1 teaspoon per 600 ml) and cook for 4 minutes or until just tender, then drain and refresh under running cold water. Crush 1 small garlic clove on a board with a little salt into a smooth paste, then transfer to a small bowl and stir in 2 tablespoons lemon juice, 3 tablespoons extra virgin olive oil, 2 tablespoons chopped parsley and 4 thinly sliced spring onions. Toss with the green beans, adjust the seasoning if necessary and leave to marinate at room temperature for 30 minutes. *Serves 4.*

Steamed rice

Wash 350 g long-grain rice in a few changes of cold water until the water stays relatively clear. Drain, tip into a 20-cm heavy-based saucepan and add $1/2$ teaspoon salt and 600 ml boiling water. Quickly bring to the boil, stir once, cover with a tight-fitting lid and reduce the heat to low. Cook for 15 minutes. Uncover, fluff up the grains with a fork, and serve. *Serves 4.*

Buttery rice pilaf

Wash 350 g long-grain rice in a few changes of cold water until the water stays relatively clear. Drain well. Melt 15 g butter in a 20-cm heavy-based saucepan, add 2 finely chopped shallots and cook gently until soft but not browned. Stir in a bay leaf and the rice and fry gently for 1 minute. Add 600 ml *Chicken stock* (see page 208) and 1 teaspoon salt and quickly bring to the boil. Stir once, cover with a tight-fitting lid and cook over a low heat for 15 minutes. Uncover, remove the bay leaf and fluff up the grains with a fork before serving.

Serves 4.

Vanilla ice cream

Slit open 2 vanilla pods and scrape out the seeds with the tip of a knife. Put 500 ml full-cream milk, the vanilla pods and seeds into a non-stick pan and bring to the boil, then remove from heat and set aside for 30 minutes to infuse the milk with the flavour of the vanilla. Put 6 egg yolks and 200 g caster sugar into a large bowl and, using an electric hand-held whisk, whisk for 3 minutes until pale and moussey. Bring the milk back to the boil, strain onto the egg yolk mixture and mix until well combined. Return to the pan and cook over a low heat, stirring, for 3–4 minutes until the mixture lightly coats the back of a wooden spoon, but do not let the mixture boil or it will curdle. Remove from the heat and set aside to cool slightly, then stir in 500 ml single or double cream and 1 teaspoon vanilla extract. Chill until cold. Pour the chilled mixture into a shallow container and freeze until almost but not quite firm. Then scrape the mixture either into a bowl or a food processor and beat until smooth, then return it to the container and freeze once more. Repeat this process 2–3 times, until the mixture is very smooth, then leave until frozen. Use as required.

Serves 4.

Other salads and side dishes

Basics

All the stocks below will be much intensified if the strained stock is then simmered with 225–450 g fish or chicken fillet, in the case of fish stock or chicken stock respectively, or shin of beef with beef stock. I quite often combine chicken stock with fish stock for stronger-flavoured fish sauces.

Fish stock
Fumet
You can also make this with 500 g cheap white fish fillet (such as whiting or coley) cut into 2 cm slices, instead of the bones, for a deeper-flavoured stock. *Makes approx. 1.2 litres*

1 onion, chopped
1 fennel bulb, chopped
100 g celery, sliced
100 g carrot, chopped
25 g white button mushrooms, sliced
1 sprig of thyme
2.25 litres water
1 kg flat fish bones, such as lemon
   sole, brill and plaice

Put all the ingredients except the fish bones into a large pan, bring just to the boil and simmer very gently for 20 minutes. Add the fish bones (or fish fillet), bring back to a simmer, skimming off any scum as it rises to the surface, and simmer for a further 20 minutes. Strain through a sieve into a clean pan, and simmer a little longer if necessary until reduced to about 1.2 litres. Use or store as required.

Chicken stock
Use the bones from a roasted chicken for a slightly deeper-flavoured stock. *Makes approx. 1.75 litres*

Bones from a 1.5-kg uncooked chicken,
   or 450 g chicken wings or
   drumsticks
1 large carrot, chopped
2 celery sticks, sliced
2 leeks, cleaned and sliced
2 fresh or dried bay leaves
2 sprigs of thyme
2.25 litres water

Put all the ingredients into a large pan and bring just to the boil, skimming off any scum from the surface as it appears. Leave to simmer very gently for 2 hours – it is important not to let it boil as this will force the fat from even the leanest chicken and make the stock cloudy. Strain the stock through a sieve and leave it to simmer a little longer to concentrate in flavour if necessary, then use or store (in the refrigerator or freezer) as required.

Beef stock
Makes approx. 2.4 litres

2 tablespoons sunflower oil (optional)
2 celery sticks
2 carrots
2 onions
900 g shin of beef
5 litres water
2 bay leaves
2 sprigs of thyme
1 tablespoon salt

For a pale brown stock, put all the ingredients except for the bay leaves, thyme and salt into a large saucepan and bring to the boil, skimming off any scum. Reduce the heat and simmer for 2½ hours, adding the salt and herbs 15 minutes before the end.

For a deeper, richer-coloured stock, heat the sunflower oil in the pan, add the vegetables and beef and fry for 10–15 minutes until nicely browned, before adding the water, herbs and salt.

Beurre fondue

This sauce is good for serving with any poached or grilled fish. You can add a tablespoon of chopped herbs of your choice if you wish.

100 g chilled unsalted butter, cut into small dice
1 shallot, finely chopped
50 ml dry white wine
50 ml water or *Fish stock* (see page 208)
Salt and freshly ground white pepper

Melt 15 g butter in a small, non-aluminium pan. Add the shallot and cook gently for 5 minutes, until softened but not browned. Add the wine and boil until reduced to 1 tablespoon, then add the water or fish stock and bring to a fast boil. Whisk in the rest of the chilled butter pieces, a few at a time. Season to taste and serve.

Hollandaise sauce

This sauce is best used as soon as it is made but it will hold for up to 2 hours if kept covered in a warm place, such as over a pan of warm water.
Serves 4

2 tablespoons water
2 egg yolks
225 g *Clarified butter* (see page 210), warmed
Juice of $\frac{1}{2}$ lemon ($1\frac{1}{2}$ tablespoons)
A good pinch of cayenne pepper
$\frac{3}{4}$ teaspoon salt

Put the water and egg yolks into a stainless-steel or glass bowl set over a pan of simmering water, making sure that the base of the bowl is not touching the water. Whisk until voluminous and creamy.

Remove the bowl from the pan and gradually whisk in the clarified butter until thick. Then whisk in the lemon juice, cayenne pepper and salt.

Variations

Béarnaise sauce

Put 1 tablespoon chopped tarragon, 2 finely chopped shallots, 20 turns of black pepper and 50 ml white wine vinegar into a small pan. Boil rapidly until reduced to 1 tablespoon. Stir into 1 quantity of Hollandaise sauce.

Quick hollandaise sauce

Using the same quantities as for Hollandaise sauce, put the water, egg yolks and lemon juice into a liquidizer. Turn on the machine and then slowly pour in the warm, clarified butter through the lid. Season with cayenne pepper and salt.

Mayonnaise

This recipe includes instructions for making mayonnaise in the liquidizer and also for making it by hand. It is lighter when made mechanically because the process uses a whole egg, whereas handmade mayonnaise is softer and richer. You can use either sunflower oil or olive oil, or a mixture of the two if you prefer. Homemade mayonnaise will keep, covered, in the fridge for up to 1 week.
Makes 300 ml

1 egg or 2 egg yolks
2 teaspoons white wine vinegar
$\frac{1}{2}$ teaspoon salt
300 ml sunflower oil or olive oil

To make the mayonnaise by hand: first make sure all the ingredients are at room temperature before you start. Put the egg yolks, vinegar and salt into a mixing bowl and then rest the bowl on a cloth to stop it slipping. Lightly whisk to break the yolks. Using a wire whisk, beat the oil into the egg mixture a few drops at a time until you have incorporated it all. Once you have added the same volume of oil as the original mixture of egg yolks and vinegar, you can add the oil a little more quickly.

To make the mayonnaise in a machine: put the whole egg, vinegar and salt into a liquidizer or food processor. Turn on the machine and then slowly add the oil through the hole in the lid until you have a thick emulsion.

Mustard mayonnaise

Make the mayonnaise above in a liquidizer using a whole egg, 1 tablespoon white wine vinegar, 1 tablespoon English mustard, $\frac{3}{4}$ teaspoon salt, a little white pepper and sunflower oil.

Aïoli

Makes 175 ml

4 garlic cloves, peeled
$\frac{1}{2}$ teaspoon salt
1 medium egg yolk
2 teaspoons lemon juice
175 ml extra virgin olive oil

Put the garlic cloves onto a chopping board and crush them under the blade of a large knife. Sprinkle them with the salt and then work them with the knife blade into a smooth paste. Scrape the garlic paste into a bowl and add the egg yolk and the lemon juice. Using an electric hand mixer, whisk everything together and then very gradually whisk in the olive oil to make a thick mayonnaise-like mixture.

Rouille
Makes about 300 ml

25 g slice day-old crustless white
  bread
A little *Fish stock* (see page 208) or
  water
3 fat garlic cloves, peeled
1 egg yolk
250 ml olive oil

For the harissa:
1 *Roasted red pepper* (see page 210)
1 teaspoon tomato purée
1 teaspoon ground coriander
A pinch of saffron strands
2 medium-hot red chillies, stalks
  removed and roughly chopped
$1/4$ teaspoon cayenne pepper
$1/2$ teaspoon salt

For the harissa, put the roasted red pepper flesh, tomato purée, ground coriander, saffron, chillies, cayenne pepper and $1/4$ teaspoon of the salt into a food processor and blend until smooth. Transfer to a bowl.

  For the rouille, cover the slice of bread with the fish stock or water and leave to soften. Squeeze out the excess liquid and put the bread into the food processor with 2 tablespoons of the harissa, the garlic, egg yolk and remaining $1/4$ teaspoon salt. Blend until smooth.

  With the machine still running, gradually add the oil until you have a smooth, thick mayonnaise-like mixture.

This will store in the fridge for up to 1 week.

Clarified butter
Place the butter in a small pan and leave it over a very low heat until it has melted. Then skim off any scum from the surface and pour off the clear (clarified) butter into a bowl, leaving behind the milky white solids that will have settled on the bottom of the pan.

Beurre manié
Blend equal quantities of softened butter and plain flour together into a smooth paste. Cover and keep in the fridge until needed. It will keep for the same period of time as butter.

Marchand du vin butter
Makes approx. 115 g

115 g unsalted butter, at room
  temperature
90 g peeled shallots, finely chopped
300 ml red wine (such as a Cabernet
  Sauvignon)
80 ml *Chicken stock* (see page 208)
$1/2$ teaspoon caster sugar
1 sprig of thyme
Salt and freshly ground black pepper

Melt 15 g of the butter in a small pan, add the shallots and cook gently until softened. Add the red wine, chicken stock and sugar and leave to simmer gently until the mixture is thick and syrupy. Add the thyme sprigs and simmer for a further 5 minutes until the mixture is thick and well reduced. Leave to cool, then remove the thyme and beat into the remaining softened butter with $1/2$ teaspoon salt and plenty

of freshly ground black pepper. Put onto a large sheet of clingfilm and shape into a log, about 2.5–3 cm thick. Wrap in the clingfilm and chill or freeze until needed.

Roasted red peppers
Either spear the stalk end on a fork and turn the pepper in the flame of a gas burner or blowtorch until the skin has blistered and blackened. Alternatively, roast the pepper in the oven preheated to 220°C/Gas Mark 7 for 20 minutes, turning once, until the skin is black. Remove from the oven. Seal the blackened pepper in a plastic bag and leave to cool. Then break it in half, remove the stalk and seeds and peel away the blackened skin. The flesh is now ready to use.

Persillade
2 garlic cloves
20 g flat-leaf parsley leaves

Peel the garlic cloves and chop quite finely, then add the parsley leaves and continue to chop them together until you have a very fine mixture.

Fresh salted cod
Sprinkle salt over the base of a plastic container in a layer 1 cm deep. Put a thick piece of unskinned cod fillet (taken from the head end of a large fish) on top and then completely cover it in another thick layer of salt. Cover and refrigerate overnight. By the next day, the salt will have turned to brine. Remove the cod from the brine and rinse it under cold water. Cover with fresh water and leave to soak for 1 hour. It is now ready to use.

Rich shortcrust pastry

225 g plain flour
$\frac{1}{2}$ teaspoon salt
65 g chilled butter, cut into pieces
65 g chilled lard, cut into pieces
1$\frac{1}{2}$–2 tablespoons cold water

Sift the flour and salt into a food processor or a mixing bowl. Add the pieces of chilled butter and lard and work together until the mixture looks like fine breadcrumbs. Stir in the water with a round-bladed knife until it comes together into a ball, turn out onto a lightly floured work surface and knead briefly until smooth. Roll out on a little more flour and use as required.

Sweet pastry

175 g plain flour
A small pinch of salt
50 g icing sugar
100 g chilled butter, cut into pieces
1 egg yolk
1–1$\frac{1}{2}$ teaspoons cold water

Sift the flour, salt and icing sugar together into a food processor or bowl, add the pieces of chilled butter and work together briefly until the mixture looks like fine breadcrumbs. Stir in the egg yolk and enough water until the mixture starts to come together into a ball, then turn out onto a lightly floured surface and knead briefly until smooth. Use as required.

Melba toast

Simply toast medium-thick slices of bread under a medium-high grill until lightly golden on both sides. Put onto a board and slice off the crusts, then put your hand on top of each slice in turn and slice horizontally through the soft bread in the middle. Cut each square into 2 triangles and grill, uncooked side up, for a few seconds more until crisp and golden. Remove and leave to cool.

Other sauces etc.

Sauce mignonette (for shellfish, see page 42)
Champagne sabayon (see page 90)
Beurre noisette (see page 94)
Beurre blanc (see page 109)
Sauce gribiche (see page 122)
Garlic butter (see page 166)

Conversion charts

Liquid measures

15 ml	$\frac{1}{2}$ fl oz
20 ml	$\frac{3}{4}$ fl oz
25 ml	1 fl oz
35 ml	$1\frac{1}{4}$ fl oz
40 ml	$1\frac{1}{2}$ fl oz
50 ml	2 fl oz
60 ml	$2\frac{1}{4}$ fl oz
65 ml	$2\frac{1}{2}$ fl oz
85 ml	3 fl oz
100 ml	$3\frac{1}{2}$ fl oz
120 ml	4 fl oz
150 ml	5 fl oz ($\frac{1}{4}$ pint)
175 ml	6 fl oz
200 ml	7 fl oz
250 ml	8 fl oz
275 ml	9 fl oz
300 ml	10 fl oz ($\frac{1}{2}$ pint)
325 ml	11 fl oz
350 ml	12 fl oz
375 ml	13 fl oz
400 ml	14 fl oz
450 ml	15 fl oz ($\frac{3}{4}$ pint)
475 ml	16 fl oz
500 ml	17 fl oz
550 ml	18 fl oz
575 ml	19 fl oz
600 ml	1 pint (20 fl oz)
750 ml	$1\frac{1}{4}$ pints
900 ml	$1\frac{1}{2}$ pints
1 litre	$1\frac{3}{4}$ pints
1.2 litres	2 pints
1.25 litres	$2\frac{1}{4}$ pints
1.5 litres	$2\frac{1}{2}$ pints
1.6 litres	$2\frac{3}{4}$ pints
1.75 litres	3 pints
2 litres	$3\frac{1}{2}$ pints
2.25 litres	4 pints
2.5 litres	$4\frac{1}{2}$ pints
2.75 litres	5 pints
3.4 litres	6 pints
3.9 litres	7 pints
4.5 litres	8 pints
5 litres	9 pints

Solid measures

5 g	$\frac{1}{8}$ oz
10 g	$\frac{1}{4}$ oz
15 g	$\frac{1}{2}$ oz
20 g	$\frac{3}{4}$ oz
25 g	1 oz
40 g	$1\frac{1}{2}$ oz
50 g	2 oz
65 g	$2\frac{1}{2}$ oz
75 g	3 oz
90 g	$3\frac{1}{2}$ oz
100 g	4 oz ($\frac{1}{4}$ lb)
120 g	$4\frac{1}{2}$ oz
135 g	$4\frac{3}{4}$ oz
150 g	5 oz
165 g	$5\frac{1}{2}$ oz
175 g	6 oz
185 g	$6\frac{1}{2}$ oz
200 g	7 oz
215 g	$7\frac{1}{2}$ oz
225 g	8 oz ($\frac{1}{2}$ lb)
250 g	9 oz
275 g	10 oz
300 g	11 oz
350 g	12 oz ($\frac{3}{4}$ lb)
375 g	13 oz
400 g	14 oz
425 g	15 oz
450 g	1 lb (16 oz)
550 g	$1\frac{1}{4}$ lb
750 g	$1\frac{1}{2}$ lb / $1\frac{3}{4}$ lb
1 kg	$2\frac{1}{4}$ lb
1.25 kg	$2\frac{1}{2}$ lb / $2\frac{3}{4}$ lb
1.5 kg	3 lb / $3\frac{1}{4}$ lb / $3\frac{1}{2}$ lb
1.75 kg	4 lb / $4\frac{1}{4}$ lb
2 kg	$4\frac{1}{2}$ lb / $4\frac{3}{4}$ lb
2.25 kg	5 lb / $5\frac{1}{4}$ lb
2.5 kg	$5\frac{1}{2}$ lb / $5\frac{3}{4}$ lb
2.75 kg	6 lb
3 kg	7 lb
3.5 kg	8 lb
4 kg	9 lb
4.5 kg	10 lb
5 kg	11 lb
5.5 kg	12 lb

Linear measures

3 mm	$\frac{1}{8}$ inch
5 mm	$\frac{1}{4}$ inch
1 cm	$\frac{1}{2}$ inch
2 cm	$\frac{3}{4}$ inch
2.5 cm	1 inch
3 cm	$1\frac{1}{4}$ inch
4 cm	$1\frac{1}{2}$ inch
4.5 cm	$1\frac{3}{4}$ inch
5 cm	2 inches
6 cm	$2\frac{1}{2}$ inches
7.5 cm	3 inches
9 cm	$3\frac{1}{2}$ inches
10 cm	4 inches
13 cm	5 inches
15 cm	6 inches
18 cm	7 inches
20 cm	8 inches
23 cm	9 inches
25 cm	10 inches
28 cm	11 inches
30 cm	12 inches (1 foot)

Oven temperatures

Gas	°C	Fan °C	°F	Oven temp.
$\frac{1}{4}$	110	90	225	Very cool
$\frac{1}{2}$	120	100	250	Very cool
1	140	120	275	Cool or slow
2	150	130	300	Cool or slow
3	160	140	325	Warm
4	180	160	350	Moderate
5	190	170	375	Moderately hot
6	200	180	400	Fairly hot
7	220	200	425	Hot
8	230	210	450	Very hot
9	240	220	475	Very hot

Index

Bibliography

Alexander, Stephanie, *Cooking & Travelling in South-West France*
  (Penguin Books Australia, 2002)
Conran, Caroline, *Under the Sun* (Pavilion Books, 2002)
Cooking with Pomiane, edited and translated from the French by Peggie
  Benton (Bruno Cassirer, 1962)
Cuisine du Terroir, edited for the English edition by Sue Lermon and
  Simon Mallet (Blenheim House Publishing, 1987)
David, Elizabeth, *French Country Cooking* (Michael Joseph, 1951)
David, Elizabeth, *French Provincial Cooking* (Michael Joseph, 1960)
Escoffier, Auguste, *Ma Cuisine* (Flammarion, 1965)
Guérard, Michel, *Cuisine Gourmande* (Macmillan, 1978)
Harbutt, Juliet, *Cheese* (Mitchell Beazley, 1999)

Harris, Henry, *Harvey Nichols, The Fifth Floor Cookbook* (Fourth Estate, 1998)
Hill, Kate, *A Culinary Journey in Gascony* (Ten Speed Press, 1995)
Koffman, Pierre, *Memories of Gascony* (Pyramid Books, 1990)
Levy, Faye, *Fresh from France* (E.P Dutton, 1987)
McGee, *On Food & Cooking – An Encyclopedia of Kitchen Science,
  History and Culture* (Hodder and Stoughton, 2004)
Olney, Richard, *A Provençal Table* (Pavilion Books, 1995)
Saveur Cooks Authentic French, by the editors of *Saveur* magazine
  (Chronicle Books, 1999)
Wells, Patricia, *At Home in Provence* (Kyle Cathie, 1997)
Wells, Patricia, *Bistro Cooking* (Kyle Cathie, 1989)
Willan, Anne, *French Regional Cooking* (Hutchinson, 1983)